T0148129

FROM GRIEF
TO GOD

A Journey of Discovery or
How I Found Myself

Gareth W. Phillips

BALBOA.
PRESS

A DIVISION OF HAY HOUSE

Copyright © 2018 Gareth W. Phillips.

All rights reserved. No part of this book may be used or reproduced by any means, graphic, electronic, or mechanical, including photocopying, recording, taping or by any information storage retrieval system without the written permission of the author except in the case of brief quotations embodied in critical articles and reviews.

Balboa Press books may be ordered through booksellers or by contacting:

Balboa Press
A Division of Hay House
1663 Liberty Drive
Bloomington, IN 47403
www.balboapress.com
1 (877) 407-4847

Because of the dynamic nature of the Internet, any web addresses or links contained in this book may have changed since publication and may no longer be valid. The views expressed in this work are solely those of the author and do not necessarily reflect the views of the publisher, and the publisher hereby disclaims any responsibility for them.

The author of this book does not dispense medical advice or prescribe the use of any technique as a form of treatment for physical, emotional, or medical problems without the advice of a physician, either directly or indirectly. The intent of the author is only to offer information of a general nature to help you in your quest for emotional and spiritual well-being. In the event you use any of the information in this book for yourself, which is your constitutional right, the author and the publisher assume no responsibility for your actions.

Any people depicted in stock imagery provided by Getty Images are models, and such images are being used for illustrative purposes only.
Certain stock imagery © Getty Images.

Print information available on the last page.

ISBN: 978-1-5043-9306-5 (sc)
ISBN: 978-1-5043-9307-2 (e)

Library of Congress Control Number: 2018902569

Balboa Press rev. date: 02/28/2018

Contents

For Tina Dawn Phillips, Marie Phillips,
and my mother, Rosa Phillips.

Acknowledgments

A big thank-you to everyone at the Aberdare Spiritualist Church, especially Netta Smart, Lyn Lewis, and Keith Walters.

And to my friends Hayley Evans and Pauline Williams—who are both members of our healing circle.

Also, thank you to John, whose brain I picked relentlessly when I was starting out on my spiritual path.

To Dai Banda for his unfailing sense of humor, Peter Webb for his help, and to my brother-in-law Alan King for helping me get through the early days after my first wife, Tina, had left her earthly shell behind.

To my family, who helped me when I was almost ready to give in—my mother, Rosa; Aunt Margaret; and Uncle Alan.

To all those wonderful people who run spiritualist churches, and to the mediums who give up so much of their time to help those who are in need.

And to all the family members and guides who have helped me so much from the world of spirit.

And finally, and most importantly to my wife, Marie, who has made my life worth living again.

Introduction

I was born in 1952 in a small town called Aberdare in the South Wales Valleys, about twenty miles from the Welsh capital of Cardiff. I met my first wife, Tina, when I was twenty years old. We were married for thirty-four years, and I told her every day that I loved her. I never took her love for granted, or at least I hope I didn't. When I said, "I love you," Tina always replied, "I love you, too." She never initiated; instead, she always replied. I think she needed to hear me say it first.

During the last few weeks of a very long and painful illness that lasted for over seventeen years, Tina said, "I love you, Gareth," for the first time without me saying it first. It made me smile with great pleasure to hear her say those words. Of course, I would reply, "I love you, too," and sometimes, "I love me, too," which always made her smile. After much thought about this, I have come to believe that my lovely girl knew she was entering the last weeks of her life, and I believe she wanted me to know how much she loved me.

I believe the paths of our lives are imprinted on our souls even though we have free will, and as Tina neared her time, she began to understand the messages she was getting. She realized that our time together was running out. This was not intuition but her soul letting her know that it was almost time to leave this life of pain. The love of my life did not want to leave me without letting me know how much I had meant to her.

I will always miss Tina. She was my whole life, and her passing devastated me so much that at one point I almost went insane with grief. But I now hope that the darkest days of my life are in the past. I have been told that I have a long road to travel, and I hope I will not walk it alone.

I know it's a very strange thing to say, but the worst event in my life has led me to become far more spiritual than I ever was before. Finding the spiritualist church in Aberdare has changed me forever. I know Tina would not want me to be sad and lonely, because she has told me so on many occasions since her passing. She has told me that she wants only love and joy for my future, the same love and joy that she had brought to my life when we were together. She has also told me that there is someone waiting for me, someone with whom I will spend the rest of my life.

CHAPTER 1

My Darkest Hour

Tina passed in July 2007. Within a year my remaining family life started to fall apart. My brother, Clive, who lived with my mother all his life was suffering with several health problems, and later we were told that he had a very severe form of Parkinson's disease. My mother, Rosa, struggled to help my brother. My uncle Alan had heart, kidney, and other serious problems and found it hard to get out and about. And around this time, my aunt Margaret was told she had cancer. Uncle Alan and Aunt Margaret have always been very caring and loving people who would do anything they could to help. But because of their own problems, they were unable to help much.

I was still struggling very badly with grief after losing Tina, and because of this, the extra burden weighed me down quite heavily. I had already tried to take my own life on two occasions after losing her. I was stopped on the first occasion by my grandmother from spirit, and Tina stopped me on the second occasion. I was later told by a medium that I was given a second chance because I had work to do for spirit.

My mother struggled very badly with grief and depression after my brother's death in 2015 and was beginning to show signs of dementia. Uncle Alan passed away at the very start of 2016, followed eleven months later by Aunt Margaret. She had battled cancer for a few years, and I think she gave up that battle after my uncle died. I must say a big thank-you to all my aunty and uncle's friends and neighbors who helped at that time, especially Jayne, Kaye, and Rose, who took quite a bit of the weight off my shoulders.

At a time when I felt I was cursed, everything changed when I met my eventual wife-to-be, Marie. She made me feel alive again. After being close friends for years, our relationship turned into love. I can now see a little clearer than I could back then, and I know I have been blessed, not cursed, by having a life with two incredibly loving women whom I have loved and who have loved me.

Sometimes in your darkest hour, a flickering light will begin to shine. Follow that light, and you will not be disappointed.

Death Is an Illusion

About ten months after the death of my wife Tina, I found the spiritualist church in Aberdare. When I walked through the doors of the Saint John Ambulance Hall, I was almost ready to give up on life.

The only thing that had kept me going up until that point was the fact that I knew Tina had never left my side. She had let me know in no uncertain terms that she would never leave me: After not being able to sleep for the first few weeks after her passing, something wonderful happened to me. Tina got into bed with me and cuddled up behind me. I was not allowed to see her, but I could feel her presence giving me the help I needed and allowing me to finally drift off to sleep. This didn't just happen on one night; it happened every single night for about four weeks. On her last visit, she didn't get into bed with me but kissed me good-bye for now. Tina got me through the worst of it, and I'm not sure I would still be here without her love and support.

But her support didn't end there. Things were being moved around in my home, and the lights and TV flickered on and off. I also heard her call my name quite often. These things gave me hope and kept me going. Because of this, I knew I needed to find out more about the afterlife. That's why I entered the spiritualist church for the first time.

Within a few weeks, they started a circle in the church, and I was asked to join. Since then, I haven't looked back. It wasn't long before I started getting inspirational writing from spirit. All these events happened so quickly that it has led me to believe that this was always meant to happen to me at this time in my life.

It's Never Too Late

I was fifty-six when I started receiving automatic writing and poetry. I had never previously written anything of worth in my entire life. Now I can't stop writing. The poems in this book are just a sample of the more than five hundred poems I have written during the last eight or nine years. Every poem I have written has either come from the higher realms or been inspired by them.

CHAPTER 2

Poetry through Grief

I started to get bits and pieces of poetry from spirit a few months after the messages of automatic writing. Many of the early poems were about grief. Shortly after this, I started to write poems myself, obviously aided by my guides. These earlier poems were mainly about grief, too, because of what I was going through at that time. These poems are quite dark. I make no apology for this because we all need to go through dark periods in our lives before we can find the light. And if we have never suffered through pain and loss in our earthly lives, how can we possibly understand and help others?

I spent quite a long time in the dark before I even contemplated moving forward with my life. It must have been very difficult for the people around me during those years. The only place I began to feel as if I belonged was the Aberdare Spiritualist Church. It was, and still is, open two days a week. The other five days I spent all my time wishing it were Wednesday or Sunday evening.

Once I started to learn the truth about life after death, my writing gradually changed and became more uplifting. About a year later, I started to read my poems in church, which helped with my confidence. I thought my confidence had been destroyed by what I had gone through. The main aim of a spiritualist church is to provide a place for those who are suffering through the loss of a loved one to find peace, understanding, and proof that life does go on in a far better place.

Most of the mediums who serve spiritualist churches only take a few pounds to cover their travel expenses. They get nothing else out of it except

4

the joy of helping another soul in despair and maybe a cup of tea and a piece of cake.

Abandoned

We shared so much love throughout the years,
But the latter half was filled with tears.
And we were both nearing the end of our tether
From the pain and torment we suffered together.

Most of the time it was just me and you,
So nobody knew what we went through.
And when I lost you, I fell apart.
Then something very cold entered my heart.

I didn't care anymore; I'd lost my way.
I lost all hope and had no reason to stay.
After you died, I prayed for death, too,
Because of the love I had for you.

I felt abandoned, almost always alone
With the most intense feelings I'd ever known.
I raged at God; my anger grew,
For I was bereft after losing you.

Thirty-four years as husband and wife,
And you brought so much joy to my life.
But now I felt lonely and empty inside,
And I believed the best part of me had died.

In the beginning, I felt incredibly numb.
Then the pain kicked in, and I thought I'd succumb.
But we've always believed that the soul survives,
And we don't live one but many lives.

So I hope this is true, and I'll see you again

In another life with far less pain.
So in the meantime, my memories will have to do,
Even though I still cry when I think of you.

The Man in the Mirror

Your loss has left me dazed and confused.
I feel as though I'm battered and bruised.
I wonder if grief alters DNA,
Because the person I was just faded away.

It was after your loving soul departed
That all these strange feelings started.
Now there isn't much of the old me left.
Is this what they mean by being bereft?

I'm living in darkness; I can't find the sun.
And I don't feel connected to anyone.
This face in the mirror doesn't fit my name.
Even my eyes don't look the same.

My reflection has changed; can this be me?
This person looks older; who can he be?
I seem to have aged in no time at all.
My God, there's a stranger in the mirror on my wall.

I do try to smile, but he never smiles back.
The man in the mirror, his moods are so black.
I say I'm okay, but my mouth fills with lies,
For you can't keep a secret with tears in your eyes.

I so often recoil at my own reflection
With a bitter taste of self-rejection.
But I always return, knowing that I'll see
That the man in the mirror will one day be me.

Missing You

You're always in my dreams.
You're always on my mind.
The gentle girl who stole my heart.
That loving soul who was always kind.
I hated my life without you.
It was abject misery.
I was shipwrecked on an island
After being lost at sea.
I couldn't see a future,
And I couldn't imagine a life
Without my very best friend,
Without my darling wife.
At first, I couldn't talk of you,
And I couldn't voice my fears.
I struggled to control myself
And fought back all the tears,
Though there is no shame in crying.
It releases anger and pain,
It helps to heal with time,
And it stops you going insane.
But when I cry, it's in private.
It's a solitary thing for me.
Men always hide their feelings,
And I guess that's how it must be.
But I'm starting to open up now,
And I'm talking to a friend.
And with love and understanding,
Maybe broken hearts can mend.

When I Breathe

My heart felt as though it was broken
Because you had to leave.
But I'm feeling a little better now,

And it only hurts when I breathe.
So, I'm trying to rebuild my life,
And I'm beginning to deal with the pain,
But there are still tears on my pillow
Because I'll never see you again.
If only I hadn't loved you so much,
This pain wouldn't be so intense.
But it was always all or nothing with me.
I could never sit on the fence.
It's about time someone invented a pill
To mend a broken heart
Or a medicine to dull the pain.
At least that would be a start.
This grief gnaws away at me
And seems to affect me more each day,
But it's a pain I must live with
Because it never quite goes away.
They say that time's a great healer,
And who am I to disagree?
It's only been a couple of years,
And I can only say how it feels for me.
I know it doesn't hurt as much as it did
And life must still go on while I grieve,
And I know it isn't as bad as it was,
But if only it didn't hurt when I breathe.

Self-Pity

I miss you so very much; I feel like I'm bleeding inside.
I really don't want to live this life; I wish we both had died.

I'm just a shell without you, one of the walking dead.
My heart feels like a block of ice; it's almost as cold as our bed.

I am trying to get back on my feet, but I keep falling down again.
Nothing is what it seems; the only real thing is the pain.

I seem to be playing a game, and I never get a break.
I struggle to the top of the ladder and then fall down another snake.

I hate this mindless game; I keep getting sent back to the start.
It makes me feel so empty inside, like having a black hole for a heart.

This is how it feels sometimes, when I'm in grief's cold embrace.
A smile that eventually comes to my lips rarely reaches the rest of my face.

Sometimes I feel so terribly alone. I sit staring at walls all day.
Now there's only that guy in the mirror, and I've heard everything he has to say.

I keep most of the pain hidden, safe under lock and key.
And if I talked to someone about it, what sort of man would I be?

I used to think I was strong. Well, I had to be for my wife.
Now there's nothing left but self-pity. I can't go on like this all my life.

I needed her like she needed me. We were together every day.
She was everything that was good in my life. So why did you take her away?

I know she suffered for so many years, but I needed her, couldn't you tell?
And I know you freed her from her pain, but why not free me as well?

Not a Strong Enough Word

Can I tell you something? Don't worry. It's not the story of my life.
I wouldn't want to bore you. This is about my wife.

She was ill for nearly twenty years, and the pain rarely went away.
She lost the use of all her limbs, and the pain increased day by day.

But despite the way she suffered, she took what she could from life.
She laughed when she was able. There was no one as brave as my wife.

I prayed to take her pain away, to let me have it for a while.
And though respite never came for her, she would still try to smile.

She never really complained at all. She never said, "Why me?"
And when her strength had all but gone, God then set her free.

At first, I was a very angry man. Then I began to understand
That God had freed her from all pain, when taking her by the hand.

I will never find the right words to tell anyone how I feel,
To say how much she meant to me, because none of this seems real.

I don't know if you knew my wife, and I don't know what you've heard.
I can't explain what she meant to me, for love isn't a strong enough word.

Dark Despair

I couldn't face this world,
So I locked myself away.
I sat alone in dark despair,
Dreading the dawn of each new day.
And when I tried to venture outside,
I would shake from head to toe.
Anxiety attacks became common for me.
On the other side of the door,
I was lost in my depression.
I clung to my grief
After my world was stolen from me
By death, that heartless thief.
I lost my strength and confidence.
My humour went away.
My moods were as black as anthracite
And my heart as cold as clay.
But now I know that death is a lie,
A lie that has caused so much fear,
Because you never really left my side,

And I know whenever you're near.
And since I found the spiritualist church,
I've become far more aware
That the circle of life is everlasting,
So I have said good-bye to despair.
Now, slowly but surely, my strength is returning
Because of this truth that I've found.
I know you're in a much better place, my love,
And not in some hole in the ground.

A Little Bit of Hope

There wasn't a warning, no time to adjust.
Everything in my life had just turned to dust.

Nothing was the same; everything had changed.
Who pulled the plug? Who rearranged?

The stars in their firmament refuse to shine
Now that you are no longer mine.

I can't find the sun. It rains every day.
Everything is black since you went away.

I don't hear the birdsong; they no longer sing.
It's permanent winter, with no sign of the spring.

I sit here alone. Quite often I cry.
Each day feels the same. Life is passing me by.

I can't move forward. I'm always retreating.
My whole world has changed since your heart stopped beating.

I hang on by my nails. Is there any hope left?
I live in the shadows, feeling lost and bereft.

Now strange things are happening. I have felt spirit's touch.
I can now feel a presence that loves me so much.

Is this a message from you? Am I becoming aware?
Is there reason to be hopeful? Do I really dare?

Just a flicker of light, the first for a while,
A little bit of hope, and the birth of a smile.

After My Heart Stops Beating

I found her when I was twenty years old,
The one I had always sought out.
She changed my life forever,
And of that there is no doubt.
Our love grew stronger as the years were passing,
And it seemed it would never end,
But my love succumbed to an illness
That no mortal man or woman could mend.
For the first time in my life, I prayed
But had to watch her slowly fade away.
All that happiness and all that love
Came to nothing one dark day.
Then I sat in grief and desolation,
Staring blankly at walls as time stood still.
Of pain and despair, I drank so much
And have finally had my fill.
I have cried too many tears,
And I know I must move on.
I may have buried her ashes deep,
But my loved one hasn't gone.
I feel her presence often.
She touches my face and hair
Just to show her love for me
And to remind me she's still there.
I have always known we were soul mates

And that death's sting is only fleeting.
So, I'll keep this flame burning brightly for her
Even after this heart stops beating.

The Ladder and the Pit

Everyone goes through the agony of grief at some point in his or her life.
We will all feel its sting like the razor-sharp blade of a knife.
Then we will have to deal with depression, which follows behind the sting,
And depression is a deep dark pit. It's an unforgiving thing.
I really believe it's a deep dark pit, but there's a ladder inside called grief,
Though you must climb so many rungs before finding any relief.
In the beginning, you avoid the ladder. You sit in dark despair,
Scared to move a muscle, hurting but content to stay in there.
One day you will find the ladder, but you might be too scared to climb,
So you try and try in vain, but you might have to give it more time.
You will only begin to climb by being positive and anger free,
Letting love back into your heart and ridding yourself of negativity.
And the farther you climb up the ladder, the happier you'll become.
Positive things will start to happen, and you'll no longer feel so numb.
And at the very end of your climb, you will see the clear blue sky.
Grief then becomes a bittersweet memory, which can still make you cry.
That's why grief never goes away, because it's a memory in the end,
A memory of someone you cherished, a family member or friend.
And depression is the deep dark pit, and grief is the ladder inside,
So do you want to come out of the dark? Because only you can decide.
Some people never come out of the pit; they never come through the despair.
They think they're safe in the darkness. They pretend that the ladder's not there.
But now I have found that ladder, and I'm reaching out for the sky.
I've had enough of feeling sorry for myself, so I'm waving that pit good-bye
Now I've started to climb the ladder, and I know what I'm doing is right.
I never want to see that dark place again, so I'm plotting a course for the light.

Please Dance Again

When you lose someone you love, the pain can be so intense.
Then loneliness invades your life, and from this there is no defense.
You can surround yourself with friends, but the loneliness is still inside
Because you miss that special someone, and your grief won't be denied.

You will always bear those scars; it's a wound that never heals.
And you can't explain it to someone who doesn't know how it feels.
This wound will never completely close; it will reopen time and again.
And the memory of your lost loved one will be the reason for that pain.

This pain does ease with time, but it never quite goes away.
You will wonder if it will ever leave, but never comes the day.
But in time you will learn the truth, that love keeps them at your side.
And eventually they will let you know that they live on and have not died.

And all they will want is your happiness, and for them it's the important
thing.
They would love to see you dance again and long to hear you sing.
For there is no jealousy in spirit. They would like you to live again,
Knowing that one day you will reunite in heaven and be free from any
pain.

As spirit that's all they desire; they want you to enjoy the rest of your life.
They don't wish you to sit alone with that grief that can cut you like a knife.
And never think they won't wait for you. Don't fill your head with lies.
The truth is they will always love you, and it's a love that never dies.

Yesterday

I used to wish I could go back in time
Just to see you as a child,
So I could watch you growing up,
The woman I loved that so beguiled.
I regret missing those early years,

14

That innocent time of your life.
But I must be grateful for what I had,
Such a loving and caring wife.

I've been looking at old photographs of you,
Never frowning, always smiling.
I wish I'd known that little girl,
So angelic, so beguiling.
But all I can do is daydream now
And stare at walls all day,
Trying to shut out the pain of grief,
But it refuses to go away.

And I'm having these vivid dreams
Where you're leading me by the hand,
And the colors are almost too bright for me
In a strange but beautiful land.
I know this pain will ease with time.
Well, that's what people say.
But time seems to be standing still,
And it feels like yesterday.

But I've made you a promise now
To move forward with my life.
But I will never ever stop loving
That sweet little girl who became my wife.

A Field of Stone

The rain is washing over me as I stand in this field of marble and stone.
A freezing wind is blowing, chilling me to the bone.
Green grass is all around me, silk, real, and plastic flowers,
Headstones full of memories, and so many tearful hours.

Each stone tells its story, names and dates from the past,
Family and friends who are no longer here, because flesh and bone don't last.

Gareth W. Phillips

Wiping away a silent tear, making sure that no one can see,
Paying my respects to the family who patiently wait for me.

I'm unable to be with them yet; I have things that I've promised to do.
So my destiny now awaits me before coming home to you.
I spend too much time in this place, a place of marble and stone.
Sometimes other people are there, but quite often I'm on my own.

It's stupid of me to keep coming, for I know this is not where you are.
You're not in this field of sad memories; you're in a better place by far.
Our loved ones are not really dead, and no, they do not sleep.
They are more alive than we are, so why in God's name do we weep?

Well, we weep because we miss them, and we feel sad because we care.
We grieve because we can't see them, even though we know they are there.
Our relationship has changed now, and we can't help but feel alone,
Because they have become pure spirit and we still have flesh and bone.

Even though we know they live on, and we know they will never leave,
We still can't help shedding tears for them, for there is a need to grieve.
But remember they no longer have pain and can do whatever they please.
They're in a better place than we are and can come and go like the breeze.

CHAPTER 3

Automatic Writing

I was told in the circle that I would start to receive writing from spirit, and not long after, I received the message immediately below, as well as the messages on the pages that follow.

Message Received

Revelations are coming for those who are willing to listen.
Do not close your ears to what we are telling you. Write it down.
Life is not supposed to be a bowl of cherries. If it were, we would learn nothing.
You will get your messages in small chunks, so you will be able to understand.
In time the amount you will be given will increase.

The Wisdom of Spirit

- ❖ Sit quietly, be silent, and eventually you will hear the truth.
- ❖ He who is loudest isn't always right.
- ❖ Be at peace with yourself and you will be at peace with others.
- ❖ In silence, you will find great strength.
- ❖ Live in harmony, not anger.
- ❖ Allow yourself to become one with all things.
- ❖ You will find your heaven in contentment.

- ❖ When you practice empathy and love, the world will rejoice with you.
- ❖ Make yourself flow without hardness.
- ❖ Be as you were as a child, open to all things.
- ❖ Allow yourself the freedom to just be.
- ❖ See beauty in all things.
- ❖ Be a listener, not a talker.
- ❖ Don't let your ego rule your life.
- ❖ Waste is also a sin.
- ❖ Listen to what is said without interruption.
- ❖ Be gentle in your ways. Do not force.
- ❖ Love is the answer to all questions.
- ❖ Contentment is the greatest gift you will ever receive.
- ❖ To want more is to enjoy less.
- ❖ Send love in your thoughts as well as in your deeds.
- ❖ Be as a sponge; let all things flow to you without effort.
- ❖ You can only learn while you listen.
- ❖ Learn to enjoy the silence.
- ❖ Don't tell people who you are. They will know you by your actions.
- ❖ Be yourself and allow others to be who they are.
- ❖ A wish is heard without shouting.
- ❖ There is virtue in being calm and serene.
- ❖ Fight against the impulse to make a comment.
- ❖ Patience and trust bring their own rewards.

A Message from My Grandfather

Because we live in times that are advancing so quickly, man has left behind the wisdom and principles of the past. We are now in an age where we only think of the material and our own personal gratification. This is a time when the way mankind lives will have to change because we can go no further in this direction without disaster. If we do carry on in this direction, it will only lead to the destruction of mankind.

The principles we have lived by in the past have been forgotten, and mankind only lives for the things he thinks will bring him pleasure. This is not the way forward but a backward step in the evolution that the spirit world wants for mankind. God sees all and hears all and has finally decided that letting mankind have its head is not working, so he has informed his angels and man's helpers from the world of spirit that mankind needs their help more now than at any other time. Many people will now turn toward a spiritual way of life, and you, Gareth, are one of these people. You are one of many. You, along with others who are also on a spiritual path, will lead a new generation of beings to help the rest of mankind to adjust to the changes that are coming. You will be a teacher, my boy, and you will teach others the things you are being taught now. This is the reason you are asking so many questions, Gareth.

When you realize that your whole life has been leading up to this point in time, you will become more enthusiastic than you have ever been before. Your future and the future of mankind are safe. It is not going to end in a blaze of fire. But the world you live in now is going to change, and you and others will be very involved in these changes. Spirituality and the personal belief you each have in spirit is going to change the world, because it must change or die.

We are entering a time that has been foretold by spirit, a time when mankind will finally see the light. Religion will be no more, and the understanding of spirit will be universal and will change mankind forever. The people who opened your eyes will be instrumental in these changes, and you will meet others along your path who will open your eyes even further. Gareth, these are exciting times, and I know you will grab the opportunity with both hands. So, Gareth, keep asking questions, keep moving forward, and you will never be disappointed at the outcome. You need not worry about your future. It is safely in the hands of spirit.

This is because you have been chosen to do God's work here on earth, but do not let this go to your head, my boy, because there are many more who have been chosen to work alongside you. Gareth, you are one of many.

A Message from Tina

Gareth, my love, you are now beginning to understand who you truly are and what you are meant to do with the rest of your life. You may not think so now, but one day you will be able to speak like you have just done to a roomful of people. You are not ready yet, but you are far removed from the shy young man I knew and loved when we first met. Gareth, I'm so proud of you and of how far you have come in such a short time.

We all understand how you feel about being on your own, but this was necessary for you to be able to think clearly about your path, and about the true meaning of this life that we all have to go through. What you are learning now is just the start for you. We will lead you to everything you need to learn so that by meditating and by the knowledge you will find in books and on the internet, you will receive the basic building blocks, which will establish a firm foothold in truth for you.

You will become a teacher, and you will find love again in this earthly life. You will not have to travel the rest of this life alone, my love, but you did need this time of solitude to do the thinking you needed to do. So, do you understand now, my love, why you have had to wait so long in this solitude? Gareth, this is a turning point in your life, and you should remember this day and be happy with the knowledge that you are becoming a new person with a new life.

CHAPTER 4

Poetry Through Knowledge

The Never-Ending Story

Standing by a grave in the rain,
Missing a loved one so.
I used to feel so very alone,
But that was a long time ago.

I now know that life goes on
In a wonderful place we cannot see,
And I know there will be a reunion one day
When it's the right time for me.

A time for great joy, not sadness,
A time to see old friends,
A time to be reunited again
On a journey that never ends.

Some say that nothing lasts forever.
Well, what about the human soul?
Because while our bodies become dust in the wind,
Our spirit will always stay whole.

Nothing can destroy our essence.
It just moves to a higher place.

And it grows with every lifetime
And with every trial we face.

So, it's all about progression,
The growth we all strive to attain,
That always ends with the journey homeward
Before deciding to return again.

This is a never-ending story,
And we are all a part of God's great plan.
We are not just human beings;
We are more than a woman or man.

We are a part of everything that ever was.
We carry the divine spark inside.
We are powerful spirit beings.
And we are strong, so we shouldn't hide.

We are all here for the same reason.
We are all volunteers. That's a fact.
And we have chosen our very own lessons,
Right down to our final act.

And when our names are called
And we are homeward bound once more,
We will take our memories with us
At the closing of another door.

You see, we are all writing the book of our lives,
A wonderful story full of love and pain,
And each chapter ends with that journey home
To be with those we have loved again.

All the Love We Shared

All the love we shared,
All that passion, joy, and pain.
Now all that's left is a broken heart
Because I'll never see you again.

I looked after you for so long.
Then that shockwave hit me as I watched you die.
You were the only reason I had for living.
Now all I could do was cry.

Not very manly, I know,
But grief doesn't take prisoners, you see.
Though at least I wept in private,
For inside those four walls there was only me.

In the past, I focused on you so much
That I actually forgot about me.
Then those prison doors were opened,
But I didn't want to be free.

No one knows what I went through,
Hiding behind that locked door.
I stayed far away from the outside world.
I didn't want this life anymore.

I prayed every day, "God take me now.
I can't function. This machine is dying."
And if I had said I hadn't given up the ghost,
Then you would have known I was only lying.

I'd spent all those years looking after you,
And eventually it had taken its toll,
Not only on my physical body
But on my heart and soul.

I had never asked you for much, Father,
So I asked you then to let me be with my wife.
"Don't let me suffer like this anymore.
Please end this bloody useless life."

But you ignored all my prayers, Father,
All the pleading to end my pain.
Instead you gave me a new life,
Something to live for again.

I found the spiritualist church,
So now I'm employed by you.
My eyes have been opened to the truth,
And I can see now what I am meant to do.

And as I became more optimistic,
Feeling a little happier day by day,
Good things started to happen again.
Now Mr. Negative has gone away.

Then seven years later, the unthinkable occurred.
I fell head over heels in love
With someone who was waiting for me,
A little present from above.

Father, I'm so glad you didn't listen to me,
Because you obviously knew what lie ahead.
Instead of finding a new reason to live,
I could quite easily have been dead.

So, Father, thank you for ignoring me,
And I'll do my best to make you proud.
I'll put this story down on paper
And then shout your praises out loud.

Wishing My Life Away

Every day without you hurts. Every week is a life sentence.
I'd do anything to be with you, and I would have no repentance.

But I can't contemplate ending my life; I'm told I have no right.
The end should come quite naturally, before seeing that heavenly light.

I know I shouldn't pray for death; this isn't the way it should be.
But sometimes in my desolation, the blackness envelops me.

So now I'm marking time. I stand rooted like a tree
I'm in suspended animation until you come to set me free.

Minutes seem like hours. I sit here counting them all.
And the clock is getting louder as it mocks me from the wall.

If I only had a magic wand, I would simply make time race
While looking in the mirror, watching lines appear on my face.

Hours would pass in seconds, and time would start to fly,
And as my end approached, to this life I would say good-bye.

And when my pain is over and I'm again in your embrace,
It would take a multitude of angels to wipe the smile from my face.

A Charmed Existence

We are spiritual beings in a human host,
Living in a body that will eventually fail.
From the day of its birth, this body will decay,
And nothing can stop it from reaching that day.
As its candle of life decreases,
Its flame doesn't burn so bright.
It will always diminish as time goes by
And is finally gone in the blink of an eye.

But we are just explorers in a human shell,
Testing the waters of this earthly life,
Perpetual beings from another dimension,
Knowledge and progress our only intention.
Then death is the next great adventure we take,
Though our spirit will now be coming of age.
We lose the heaviness of our human shell
And then suddenly realize that Earth is our hell.

Though nothing can prepare us for the lightness of spirit,
For there are no restrictions at all.
Released from the bondage of an earthly existence,
We find ourselves free, without resistance.
Then we rise like a phoenix from the ashes once more,
Like a rocket breaking through the atmosphere
To be welcomed back into spiritual grace,
And find ourselves in a heavenly place.

And we forever live this charmed existence
Because as spirit we can never die.
We have always drunk from the fountain of youth,
And as God is my whiteness, this is the truth.

A Charmed Life

Are you so terribly afraid to die that you are too frightened to live?
Do you hold your possessions so tightly that you are no longer able to give?
Are you so sure in what you believe is the truth that your mind is totally closed?
Have you become so completely negative that to all new ideas you're opposed?

Do you shout your opinions too loudly; has your life become one long fight?
Are you at war with yourself and others because he who is loudest is rarely right?
Do you ignore all the beauty around you; is your life just shades of grey?

Are you blind to all of God's wonders, which can never fade away?

Does anger eat you from the inside so that you cannot sleep at night?
Do you hide away in the shadows instead of looking for the light?
Is there always something else you want; is the need for more causing you stress?
Can you be satisfied with what you have, for while you crave more, you enjoy less?

Why not be content with what you have, be gentle, and never use force?
You are a spiritual being, forever young, that will always return to the source.
Remember, hate will eventually destroy you and cause you unending strife,
While love is the answer to all questions, for love is the meaning of life.

Your immortal soul is indestructible; only your shell will feed this earth
While your soul continues upon its journey, via the usual means of death and rebirth.
So the message is, do not be afraid, have no fear, you cannot be harmed.
You were made in the image of an immortal being to live a life that's charmed.

What happens to you in this earthly life is just a learning process, my friends.
It's an endless search for knowledge and truth on a spiritual journey that never ends.
And there's a far better time to come, in a wonderful place without pain or fear,
Where no one is looked down upon by others and spiritual love is always near.

You don't have to believe me if you don't want to; you have free will. It's your choice
To live your life in fear and anger or to open your heart and rejoice,
To live a life without forgiveness, spread rumor, be hateful, and lie
Or to live a life of warmth and love before leaving your human shell to die.

Going Home

A spirit free from its prison
Is a soul from the body risen.
Like a flower opening to the sun,
A new life has begun.

But mortal man won't understand
Until he finds his neverland.
With earthly cravings left behind,
Truth and wonder he will find.

Then seeing with his spirit eyes,
Saying farewell to earthly lies,
All God's wonders no longer hidden,
All bad feelings here forbidden.

If you could see what I can see,
Earthbound you wouldn't want to be.
When the time is right you will return,
After the lessons you were meant to learn.

For this is where all life began,
The birth of woman, the birth of man,
And until we cross that great divide,
Memories of our home will be denied.

Don't be impatient. You must wait
Before you see that heavenly gate.
Then the traveler returns, no longer to roam.
That's when it hits you: heaven is home.

An Old Man's Tale

These eyes of mine don't see very clearly now,
And they're not as bright as they were when I was young.
These ears no longer pick up the slightest sound
Without the help of my hearing aid.
My hair is receding at an alarming rate,
And a multitude of wrinkles has completely changed the way I look.
My teeth no longer permanently reside in my mouth
And spend much of their time in a glass of water.
I have so many aches and pains these days
It's becoming very hard to get around like I used to.
I am definitely not the young man I used to be.
But now I'll let you in on a little secret.
I discovered this secret many years ago.
This flesh and bone is not who I am.
Deep inside me there is a light that shines so brightly.
This is my soul, which will never age
Even though it has lived many lifetimes.
And when this aging body finally releases me from its hold,
I will once again be young and vigorous,
And I will fly like a bird.
No matter how old you are,
There is always this feeling of being young at heart.
This feeling has always been there.
Everyone has this feeling.
This is your soul speaking to you,
And if you can stop all the noise inside your head
And sit in silence and listen,
You will eventually hear the truth,
That spiritually you are forever young,
And that a soul that has come into being can never die.

Pearls on a Chain

How does God know how every living thing feels?
How can something like this be true?
Surely, he can't feel everyone's pain,
And why should he care about me and you?

There are over seven billion people on this planet,
Separated by land and sea.
How can he feel all those souls?
And why should he care about me?

I was told that there's a duality to our lives
And that we are all entities that have a soul.
We are each a part of the one true God.
We are each a piece of the whole.

We are all a part of the Great Spirit,
So it's not that hard to explain.
We were all created in his loving image.
We are just like pearls on his chain.

So how do you feel when a loved one suffers?
Does having empathy leave its mark on you?
Could you have the same feelings for everyone?
Would a stranger's suffering affect you too?

When you evolve and have love for each living thing,
Then in heaven you can choose to remain.
Then you'll understand how the Great Spirit feels
About all the pearls on his chain.

The Water Cycle

High up in the mountains, a babbling brook begins to flow.
Then joined by other small waterways, its speed begins to grow.

Eventually it becomes a stream, flowing faster, flowing free.
It has one goal in life, and it knows where it must be.

Now joined by other streams, it becomes a river at last.
Onward, ever onward, nothing can stop it moving so fast.

Swift runs this little river, on its mission to reach the sea.
When it joins a bigger brother, then it has become a tributary.

Now this powerful mighty river speeds along its way.
It finally passes through an estuary, and in the ocean it will stay.

Then through our sun's great power, the water then is warmed.
With evaporation and condensation, this is how the clouds are formed.

The wind then plays its part and blows the clouds over land.
The rain then falls on the mountains again, for this is what was planned.

It fills our lakes and reservoirs, and all living things are fed by the rain.
It feeds our streams and rivers, and then the water cycle starts again.

We take this water for granted; no one thinks how it comes about.
We hardly give it any thought, unless there is a drought.

But ask yourself this question: Who designed this plan,
This miracle of engineering? Because it certainly wasn't man.

Not of This Earth

The sun is warm on my shoulders, and I can hear the birds in the trees.
I can see and smell the flowers and feel a gentle breeze.
It's one of those days you can almost taste, and I can sense spirit all around.
New life is everywhere you look, in the trees, in the bushes, and on the ground.

Springtime—what a lovely word. It just makes me want to smile.

I'm starting to feel like my old self again, and I haven't been for a while.
You know there's no better feeling than this, to be at peace with the world,
No nationalism to hide behind, no flags or banners being unfurled.

We call ourselves human beings, and I'm one of over seven billion, I'm told.
My creed and color are unimportant; when God made me, he broke the mold.
But that's because we are all different. We are all individuals. It's true.
There are never two people exactly alike. There is never another exactly like you.

So rejoice in your individuality. God doesn't want you to be a clone.
You don't need to be a follower; the path you must follow is your own.
That's why you've been given free will, to choose your very own path,
To make mistakes and learn from them, and to triumph over pain and wrath.

And to let forgiveness into your heart, banishing anger, hate, and greed.
We are meant to live with love and light. All the baser instincts, we don't need.
And being positive is essential for everyone, so that's what we need to do.
Now the penny has finally dropped with me. Is it beginning to drop with you?

But I'm not who you think I am, and I'm not who you think you see.
I'm not the person you see on the surface, and I won't be who you want me to be.
I'm the spirit and soul that lives inside, and I evolve with each rebirth.
I am not a citizen of this world; I'm a child of God, and I am not of this earth.

Forever Free

I have a riddle for you.
I'm not merely a woman or a man.
I'm not an animal, wild or tame.

Have you any idea of what I am?
I once stood at the walls of Jericho
And watched in awe as they fell.
I survived the destruction of Pompeii
And can still recall that hell.
I marched across the Alps with Hannibal
And still remember that freezing cold.
I saw Lincoln free the slaves,
Never again to be sold.
I died in the mud of Flanders Field,
Before I even became a man.
And I witnessed the bombing of Hiroshima
As a child in wartime Japan.
I was burned as a witch in my own village,
Another healer who paid the cost.
I have lived a life as a disabled child
And freely admit to feeling lost.
I helped to build the pyramids.
As a slave, I lived and died.
I watched the great prophet nailed to a cross,
And with bitter tears I cried.
I am a citizen of many different lands,
And I've sailed the seven seas.
I have seen the birth and death of nations
And the powerful brought to their knees.
I have lived so many lifetimes,
And death will never frighten me.
I have been around for eternity.
I am spirit, forever free.

Count to Ten

Never confront someone when you're angry. Try to calm your mind.
Count to ten and hold your words. Don't be bitter. Try to be kind.
I've been told that I should do this, though it's very hard to do.
You need to bite your tongue sometimes, and that can be painful, too.

Gareth W. Phillips

First, try to calm yourself; you'll be able to think things through.
Get your feelings under control. You know it's the right thing to do,
If you can leave it for a couple of days, then things won't look so black.
You can put things into perspective and get your composure back.

And when you're ready to talk, try not to raise your voice.
Search for the right words to say, and make the constructive choice.
It's easier said than done, I know, but try not to overreact.
Make sure you don't lose your temper. Maybe it's time for some tact.

And if this still doesn't help you, leave it cool down for a while.
Just agree to disagree and walk away with a smile.
Try not to hold a grudge, because hate can tear you apart.
You just need to let it go, and please don't harden your heart.

Remember to forgive and forget; it's the wisest thing to do.
For if you end up hating someone, then the one who'll be hurt is you.
So never use words as weapons, because one day old scars may heal.
All things can mend with time. People do change the way that they feel.

But if you say words that were meant to hurt, that memory will always exist,
And words that are spoken in anger will often hurt more than a fist.
So why not be a builder of bridges and let God's love be your guide,
For we are all brothers and sisters, and this should never be denied.

Don't Waste Time

On the day that you are born, your clock of life begins to tick.
So enjoy every day as if it's your last, because life can end so quick.

Don't take your time on earth for granted. Enjoy it while you may.
Live the life you were born for, and savor every day.

Don't waste a second on hate. You're choosing the hardest path.
Life will flow much easier, without all the anger and wrath.

And if you spend your time wanting more, then you will never be satisfied.
Take pleasure from what you already have. Just relax and enjoy the ride.

Because if you do find contentment, it's the greatest gift you will ever receive.
Then peace and harmony will stay by your side and hopefully never leave.

But we all want more than we have, never satisfied with what we need.
We are always chasing rainbows, but isn't that called greed?

And it's a waste of time being envious, always thinking, *This isn't fair.*
For if you love someone who returns your love, then you're rich beyond compare.

One day you will look back on your life, and there'll be things you will regret.
There'll be wishes that never came true and people you never met.

There'll be words left unsaid and opportunities you never took.
Then you will feel a little sadness, at the closing of your book.

But if you have known love and have felt its warm embrace,
Then you should always return to your maker with a smile upon your face.

Every Breath We Take

Every blade of grass,
Every single grain of sand,
The colors in a rainbow,
A newborn baby's hand;
Every crawling insect,
Every creature capable of flight,
The breathtaking beauty of a sunset,
And all the stars at night;
Every new, full, and quarter moon

And every plant that grows,
The sunrise in the morning,
The perfume of a rose;
Every cloud in the sky,
Every dewdrop and every flower,
The planets in our heavens,
And the wind with all its power;
Every single drop of rain,
Every delicate flake of snow,
All the senses that we have,
And every seed we sow;
Everyone we love,
Every river, pond, or lake,
The first cry when we're born,
And the last breath we take;
Every wagging tail,
Every creature great or small,
Even the things we're too blind to see—
The Lord God made them all.
So be grateful for what you have,
Not for what you crave,
For you can't take anything with you
When you journey beyond the grave.

A New Man in the Mirror

The man in the mirror has changed.
He no longer feels so deranged.
His essence is still there, deep inside,
Though all the bitterness has finally died.
Along with unwarranted feelings of guilt,
The man in the mirror has been rebuilt.
His physical pain is now long gone,
Along with the mental anguish that was heaped upon.
Only the loneliness can still reside
Because he misses the loving one that died.

But now he knows better because he's aware
That the one he loved is always there.
The man in the mirror is stronger at last,
Because he's tried so hard to forget his past.
A brand-new person has now emerged,
For most of the pain has finally been purged.
He looks straight in the mirror once more.
He no longer looks down at the floor.
His head is held high, for he knows his own worth.
He now understands his link to this earth.
What happened has brought many changes for the good,
And all his lessons are now understood.
He found a spiritual haven, a place of peace,
With knowledge freely given that helped him release.
He now understands he was meant to help others,
For he knows we are all sisters and brothers.
So what he has learned, he can now pass on
To those who think their loved ones have gone.
And to those who believe that death is the end,
He can say with surety you're mistaken, my friend.
Once he was blind, but now he has sight,
For the man in the mirror has seen God's light.

CHAPTER 5

Strange but True

A Trip on the Astral Plain

Just after I joined the spiritualist church, something very strange happened to me while I was sleeping. My wife Tina appeared before me, dressed in a long white gown, and she told me to take her hand and come with her because she wanted to show me where she was at that time.

All I can remember now was arriving inside the largest room I had ever seen in my life. I looked in front of me, and this huge, long room went on forever. I looked behind me, and it was the same. I could not see the end of the room. Beds lined both sides, hundreds of them. Everything was a dazzling shade of white, but this didn't seem to hurt my eyes at all. If there had been a speck of dirt, I would have seen it, but there wasn't.

Tina told me that the reason she was in this hospital was because her illness had lasted so long that her spirit and soul were depleted and needed to recover before she started her work in the spirit world. Tina introduced me to some of the patients and nurses there, and we talked for quite a while.

Then a very tall man dressed in all white approached me and told me it was time to return to my earthly body, but I didn't react well to this and told him I wanted to stay. I remember getting very upset because I didn't want to leave Tina, and this also upset her. The next thing I knew, I felt myself being drawn backward. I then woke with a jolt as if I had fallen onto the bed from a height.

I told a few members of my family, and they tried to convince me that it had just been a dream, but I knew it wasn't because it had been far too real. Then a few weeks later, I got a message in our church from a medium called George Seaton; he told me everything that had happened to me, including a description of the hospital room and the fact that I had caused a bit of a stir.

A few weeks after that, I received further proof from an elderly gentleman called John Hamer. He had gone through the exact same experience in what seemed like the same hospital. Since this happened, I have an unshakable belief in life after death, and I know there is a better life to come.

The thing I remember most from this incredible experience is the overwhelming feeling of love that surrounded me on the other side. Apart from being with my wife Tina, that is what I miss the most.

I Have Been Patient

On June 7th, 2010, I received a message from my grandfather Thomas Richards via automatic writing that said when I realized that my whole life had been leading up to this point in time, I would become more enthusiastic than I had ever been in my life. Several months before receiving that message from my grandfather, I was told something similar by two different mediums: "You have been very patient for a very long time, but you won't have to wait too much longer now."

About two weeks after receiving the message from my grandfather, I had a conversation outside the Aberdare church with a medium called Eric. He told me about the changes that were coming and said many spiritualists would be expected to teach others about them. Later that month, I bumped into Eric again at another church, and he enlightened me even more.

At the circle in early August, my friend Hayley gave me a message, and right at the end of the message, she said, "You have been very patient, but now it's your time."

Two days later, I received a message at home from Tina, and as usual, she gave me the name of a song so that I could do some research and find the hidden message in the lyrics. Tina often uses this method, knowing how much I love my music. The name of the song was Tesla Girls by

Orchestral Manoeuvres in the Dark. So I did some research and found the following lines in the lyrics:

> I've been patient, heaven knows. I've learned the rules and how it goes. I can't sit still or settle down, and my feet don't seem to touch the ground.

Then, in something I found later in a discussion forum on the internet called, this is the time of the Quickening, By Tony Crisp, I found these words about the future of mankind:

> Many of you have been waiting for this since you were children. All the time within you has lived an empty place that has not been filled by the pastimes that life has offered. Nor has it been given light by the words emerging from temples and churches. For it was not for these you were born or waiting, and although the sense of that empty place never left you, and scraps of knowing arose in your thoughts, yet it was never clearly spoken.

This made me think about my childhood. I had never felt very connected to anyone, and I often felt like an outsider. I never followed the trends that most of my friends followed. I dressed the way I wanted to dress and did what I wanted to do. In fact I was never a follower or trendy.

At one time, I mistakenly thought I might have been adopted. This feeling was initiated by my brother telling me that my parents loved him more than me because I was adopted. I also never felt the need to go to church or read the Bible, despite both sides of my family being deeply religious. Yet I have always believed in God, reincarnation, and the place we call heaven. It was as if I knew even as a child that religion was not meant for me. Then, in April 2008, I found the spiritualist church, and after learning more about this way of life, I realized that I had been a spiritualist all my life and that, therefore, I had no need of a religion or any of the dogma that comes with it.

The day I wrote these words onto my pad, the weather was shocking. The rain hadn't let up all day, and there hadn't even been a break in the cloud cover. As I wrote the last words and closed the pad, suddenly the sun shone through my window, almost blinding me with a burst of brightness, illuminating this moment of personal clarity. Believe it or not, the sunlight only lasted for about ten seconds and then the Welsh weather carried on doing what it does best.

I'm Not Alone and Never Have Been

Ever since the death of my beloved wife Tina in 2007, I have hated Christmas festivities and have looked upon the coming of each New Year with great trepidation. When I lost my wife, I lost everything. Tina wasn't just my wife; she was my soul mate and best friend.

And because I had been caring for her for the better part of twenty years, I suppose I had also lost what I regarded as my job. My car was a mobility car, so that went very quickly as well, though the only thing that mattered to me at that time was the loss of my lovely Tina.

Then on New Year's Eve in 2010, something incredible happened to me while I was watching the start of the New Year on the television. A few minutes after the clock struck twelve, my living room was suddenly filled with a mist that seemed to be full of little lights buzzing around like a swarm of midges on a summer night.

I couldn't believe it. I had my very own fireworks display in my living room, one that was far superior to anything I had just seen on my television screen. Not only could I see these little lights, but I could also feel them touching me all over and an overwhelming feeling of love surrounded me. This part of the experience lasted for around ten minutes, and I was transfixed. My mouth hung open in awe and amazement. But it didn't end there. When I got into bed later that night, the mist started swirling all around me again, and then something that had often occurred in my bedroom in the past happened once more: it started to snow indoors. In fact, a blizzard fell on me from the ceiling. When this happens, I can feel the flakes landing on me, and they seem to be absorbed into my body.

I do know it isn't really snow, though it does feel cold when it lands on my upturned face. I have often wondered what it is and why I regularly have this experience, so I have asked several medium friends about this phenomenon, but no one has come back to me with any answers yet.

When my New Year's experience was over, I rolled over and fell into a deep sleep, knowing that I was never alone and that all my loved ones from the spirit world were always very close to me. Ever since this wonderful experience, my bedroom has filled with the swirling mist almost every single night, I usually watch it before falling asleep, and if I'm lucky, I also get a bit of indoor snow.

I've also had other experiences while staring at my ceiling. Sometimes it's like watching a film being projected above me, but it's always moving too fast for me to clearly make out what's going on. Hopefully one day I can raise my vibration enough to see what the spirit world is trying to show me. I know that my helpers and guides are readying me for something, but for now, who knows what it is.

Protection from an Archangel

After seeing an angel book in a Swansea Spiritualist Church, a book that I already owned and had only just glanced at, I suddenly got the feeling that I should read it. When I got home, I opened the book to a random page, and as I looked at the drawing of the archangel Michael, I was told by one of my guides to ask for help. So I asked the archangel Michael for protection. I don't really know why I did this, because I had never done anything like this before; So I just did what I was told. After I asked for protection, I then began my meditation, and while I was in the process of meditating, I received the following message from someone I call a higher being:

> Be at peace, my child, for you are protected, for you work with the light and the love you have in your heart is for your fellow beings and not in any way for your own egotistical feelings. We understand the way you are feeling now, and we are helping you all we can. Never give up, my child, for you and others like you will one day help to change the world you live in. Be not afraid, for you are surrounded by those who love you, and often the thoughts that enter your head are ours and not yours. Live the rest of this earthly life with the confidence that we will

always be there to help you whenever you need us. You need to call on us more often now, Gareth, to help you get through this period of your earthly life, because you really do need our help now.

The following day I was involved in a car accident. My car aquaplaned on a newly laid road surface during very heavy rain. In nearly thirty years of driving, I had never had an accident, but on this occasion even though I braked in plenty of time, my car just did not stop, and I gave the car in front of me a hefty blow and was sure I had done quite a bit of damage to both cars.

But when the other driver and I looked for damage, there wasn't any, not even a scratch on either car. We looked at each other and both said it was a miracle. We then shook hands and went our separate ways.

Because I was told to ask for protection regularly and to ask other archangels for help, the very next day I asked the archangel Gabriel to give me some advice and to tell me what my spiritual path was.

The following poem is the reply I got later that day:

Be the One

Do not hesitate, do not waver, just stay on your course.
Be gentle in all you do, my son, for there is no need for force.
You have many miles to go on a road that never ends,
And all along the way you will make many new friends.
Some will stay forever, but some will come and go,
And as you make your progress, you will come to know
That what you're meant to do is a lesson you must teach
To all those who need to change and those you are meant to reach.
This is a mission from God, a mission you undertook,
A mission of love and caring, for you will write the book,
A book that others will cherish, a book that many will read,
A book that will change many lives, for many have this need.
So do not take a backward step. We are always at your side.
And never fear for your safety, because we have never lied.
You are well looked after, my boy. For the angels send their love,

Know they are always with you, protecting from above.
Just do what you were meant to do, for now you understand,
For this has been known for eons. This is what we planned.
This is a time of great change that was always meant to be,
When the earth will sing again and mankind will be free.
You will play your part, with others you will find,
To change this hurting world and free all of mankind.
Be brave, my son. Be brave, go forward, and be sure
That you are loved by many, and that love will always endure.
Be who you were meant to be and make us proud, my son.
This is your time to shine; now you must be the one.

The Following Day

The following day in the Hirwaun church near Aberdare, I was told that
the reason I needed protection from spirit was that there were so many
distractions in my life at that time that I wasn't thinking clearly. My mind
was on all the problems I had been trying to sort out with my family, a
search for work that didn't seem to exist, not to mention the problems I
was having because I spent so much time on my own.

I had also noticed that I couldn't really focus on my writing and
spiritual work. So that was the reason I'd been receiving protection from
the angels, and I have to believe that this is true.

I often get premonitions, or gut feelings, if you prefer, and then do
something that I would not normally do. For example, one day while
driving home early in the morning, I just changed my route for no reason
at all. I learned later that day that there had been a bad car accident on the
route I normally took. The road was closed for several hours at the time I
would have been traveling on it. Now, I don't say that I would have been
involved in the accident, but I would certainly have been stuck in the
ensuing traffic jam.

CHAPTER 6

More Poems

Old Age Doesn't Come Alone

Old age doesn't come on its own, they say.
And there are many who will swear to that today.
Old bones will creak, and ankles will swell,
And for many, aging can feel like hell.

The tablets and capsules in their boxes we keep
For the aches and pains that prevent our sleep,
The knees that creak when we try to rise,
The glasses we wear to aid our eyes,

The loss of hearing that was once so strong—
Oh, Father, what's happened? Where has our youth gone?
We feel our age, and it doesn't seem fair,
But then there is always someone worse off out there.

We see children playing, and we long for the day
When we used to behave in the very same way.
We see them frolic and having fun
While we struggle to walk, let alone run.

Our memories of childhood will quite often return,
And for our youth and vigor, we will sometimes yearn.

Oh, for the days when we were in our prime,
Running and skipping with no thought of time.

Now all that has gone, and I have to say
That it's sad for those who have had their day.
But, Father, couldn't we age without all the pain?
Stay youthful to the end and our vitality remain?

With everyone having their four score and ten,
Without any hardship for older women and men?
All our lives we'd be happy with bodies still strong.
With no worries about aging, we'd be happy to go on.

To still be fit at ninety with all our faculties intact,
No arthritis, and no infections in our urinary tract.
No loss of memory, and no dental decay.
Then with no need for false teeth, we could throw them away.

Then one day, Father, we would hear you say,
"Come in, number twenty, you've had your day,
And come in, sixty-three, it's time to go.
It might come as a shock, but we couldn't say no.

It's just an idea, Father, that I'm sending out there.
I'm not trying to tell you your job; I wouldn't dare.
I know it's a pipe dream, just a longing for the past,
And I know we are meant to decay and not to last.

Because we must suffer so that we may progress
Through our aches and pains, mistakes and stress.
Our lessons must be learned for the heights we attain,
But I must say, Father, getting old is a pain.

Playing with Fire

Mankind has such a lot to learn, and if you hold this to be true,
Then you are heading in the right direction and there is hope for you.

We don't have all the answers; we are as children on this earth.
Our most important lesson to learn is that every living thing has worth.

If any species becomes extinct, even if by human neglect,
This could alter the delicate balance of nature and have a far-reaching effect.

Every living thing has a purpose; they each have a task to fulfill.
We need to have respect for all living things; we need to think before we kill.

Humans are traveling at such a great speed, but we've lost our sense of direction.
We are all spiritual beings, but many haven't made the connection.

This connection must be made soon, for we cannot afford to delay.
Our planet is becoming very sick, and its problems increase by the day.

The Brazilian rainforest is being destroyed, fossil fuels are in decline,
And natural disasters are becoming more frequent. We are being sent a sign.

I'm told the polar ice is melting and that sea levels may rise.
Even the seasons are changing, so maybe it's time to open our eyes.

We systematically strip this planet, and we ignore the rules of cause and effect.
We take Mother Nature for granted, and there's a complete lack of respect.

If we choose to ignore all the signs, then the consequences will be dire.
Ignorance and greed are dangerous bedfellows, and we are playing with fire.

Attraction

So, you've had a very hard life,
And so many people have caused you pain.
Everything seems to go wrong for you,
Over and over again.
You say when is it going to end?
Will I ever catch a break?
What do I have to do to be happy?
What is it going to take?

Well, for a start stop saying, "Why me?"
Feeling like a victim makes you one.
Walking around under your own dark cloud
Means you will never see the sun.
Negative thoughts attract negative people,
And they can drag you into depression.
They can make your life a living hell,
But only if you let them.

So try to become more positive.
Then see the way your life will change.
Send out positive thoughts to the universe,
And you'll attract good things. It isn't that strange?
Send love instead of hate.
Don't let anger sour your days,
And don't send bad thoughts to others.
Try to change all your negative ways.

Learn to be forgiving,
And don't waste your time in the past.
Forget about old grievances.
Let them go. They don't have to last.
Let the past take care of itself.
Try living in the present each day

Because the future will come when it's ready.
This is the spiritual way.

And never be envious of anyone.
Be happy with what you have got.
For contentment is the greatest blessing,
And this will help you a lot.
So be positive, send love, and forgive.
Be content and live in the present.
And forget about old hurts and grudges.
Then life will become far more pleasant.

Go on, just give it a try,
And be caring in all that you do.
Then a new life and a brand new start
Will be more available to you.
It's the hidden law of attraction,
And it's the same above as it is below.
But if you don't ask, you won't receive.
Well, I just thought I'd let you know.

Remember all prayers are heard,
But the loudest are those that you pray for others,
The ones when you are being at your most selfless
By caring about your sisters and brothers.
And always remember we are all being tested
On that chosen path we travel along.
Then one day all our trials will end,
But only after they have made us strong.

Forever Young

I used to worry about getting old, but now I'm quite used to the idea
And it doesn't bother me nearly as much; old age doesn't hold so much fear.
In my mind, I can still do reckless things, but I don't think I'll give them
a try.

I understand my body's limitations now, though hopefully I'm still too young to die.

So I'll just have to grow old gracefully. Well, I don't really have much choice.
Arthritis has infected most of my body, and I often seem to lose my voice.
I still have one or two teeth, but the grinding ones are all gone.
I can chew one salted nut for an hour because there's nothing to grip it upon.

Now I'm starting to lose my hearing, though it isn't too bad yet.
And I don't have trouble remembering faces; it's the names that I forget.
I've still got all my senses, though they often don't work as they should.
There's more hair under my arms than on my head, and that does, t look very good.

Every time I stand, my knees go crack. My right elbow is just as bad.
I can walk into a room and think, *Why am I here?* And that really makes me mad.
But I've learned many things in this life, if only I could remember what they are.
And I can't complain because my legs do work. Well, only if I don't walk too far.

But I really don't fear growing old now, though I won't say it makes me glad.
I don't make the mistakes I used to. You know, growing old isn't all bad.
I'm finally learning how to relax, and I've become a more rounded being.
I understand my body more now, and I question the things that I'm seeing.

I don't rush through life with my eyes closed; I appreciate the beauty around.
And I'm finally comfortable with who I am and the new confidence that I've found.
There's bound to be a few more wrinkles, but my song hasn't yet been sung,
And even though my body is creaking a bit, my soul is forever young.

If Tomorrow Doesn't Come

What if tomorrow doesn't come?
What if this is your very last day?
Would you be ready to meet your maker?
And what would you have to say?
Are you proud of the way you've lived your life?
Could you face him without remorse?
Have you lived the life you promised?
Or did you often stray from your course?
So, if tomorrow never comes
And you must face your life review,
Could you say with total surety
That you did the very best that you could do?
Did you learn about forgiveness?
Was love at the core of your being?
Have you followed your soul's desire
Through a life of caring and feeling?
Or have you inflicted pain on others?
Have you been the cause of so much strife?
Has anger and violence been at the forefront
Of another wasted life?
Do you think you've got away scot-free?
Do you think no one has seen?
Then you've made a huge mistake, my friend,
By living a life so mean.
The spirit world sees everything.
There is nothing they don't know.
So if tomorrow never comes for you,
I sincerely hope you'll be good to go.
It'll be no use thinking, *I should have done this,*
And why did I cause so much pain?
Because after meeting your maker, my friend,
You may have to relive that life again.

Pearls of Wisdom

My mother said to me,
"Follow these rules to the end.
Always respect your partner.
She's not just your wife; she's also your friend.

"She should always be your best friend.
So never take her for granted.
Treat her with the utmost respect.
This is how the seeds of love are planted."

Mother said, "Never go to sleep after a row;
Make up before going to bed.
You will have a happy marriage,
And with luck you will always stay wed."

She said, "Never say hurtful things;
They can't be removed from the mind.
Harsh words are never forgotten.
So remember, my son, be kind."

And this piece of wisdom came from my father.
He said, "There's something I want you to know,
And this is really important, my boy:
Never eat yellow snow."

I will never forget these pearls of wisdom,
And I was very happy with my wife.
And I will always remember my mother's words,
And I avoided yellow snow all my life.

A Random Act of Kindness

A random act of kindness,
Performed with no thought of reward,

Is never missed or forgotten
By the angels of the Lord.
And with each act of kindness
Your soul is polished to a shine.
It will sparkle like a diamond
Found at the bottom of a mine.
A simple smile to an elderly person,
The opening of a door,
Just a few friendly words—
Sometimes it doesn't take more.
It may not seem like much to you,
But it could brighten up someone's day,
A little magic moment
Among all their dismay.
It doesn't have to cost you anything,
But it could mean so much to others.
Remember we are all God's children.
We are all sisters and brothers.
So for every single act of kindness
Performed while you live,
Your soul will benefit greatly
From all of the love you give.
Your life will begin to change
When you let love be your guide.
You will become blessed by our maker
And have the angels on your side.
Nothing ever goes unnoticed,
The bad as well as the good.
But there will always be a reward
For living the life we should.

Don't Make a Fuss

Don't make a fuss when I die.
Please don't mourn, and please don't cry.
Donate my parts to a worthy cause,

If they can find any bits that don't have flaws.
Medical science can have the task,
But make sure I'm dead. That's all I ask.
Don't bother with a coffin; it would be a waste.
Why cut down trees that take years to replace?
Just put what's left into some old sack.
Give the worms a treat; I'm not coming back.
Stick me in the garden and don't tell a soul,
Though promise not to frighten the mole.
So when I kick the bucket, or pop my clogs,
I'll be rid of this body that's gone to the dogs.
I won't give a damn; I'll be having a ball.
Though I'll be keeping an eye out; I'll be watching you all.
Only my body will nourish the ground,
But I won't see it. I won't stick around.
Don't worry about me. I'll be doing quite well.
I'll be happy in heaven while you're in this hell.
So, I truly don't mind if I'm someone's tea,
For there'll be nothing remaining inside that's me.
I really don't care, so do what you feel.
Give a few hungry creatures a meal.
I'll be glad to be rid of this old bag of bones
That's caused me so many aches and moans.
Back in the spirit world I won't have a need,
So give all those creatures a damn good feed.
Just put down a marker saying here's where he lies.
He liked all the insects, even the flies.
This is my legacy. This is how it should be.
So tell all the insects dinner's on me.

Now You May Stay

To love someone with all of your heart,
To wish more for them than for yourself,
To be connected to the power of spirit
Is to have something more precious than wealth.

To find the truth of your own existence,
To know you will overcome death,
To find someone who feels the same as you,
Who will love you till their very last breath,
To face all your many obstacles
And try to live with a smile,
To know we are all indestructible
And to understand that life is a trial,
To be all that you can be,
To make every dream come true,
To see inside yourself
And to know the real you,
To be of service to God and spirit,
To know that your senses have grown,
To be able to feel someone else's pain
As if it were your own,
To know your third eye has opened,
To be shown a life from your past,
To be given a glimpse of the future,
Then you'll be fully awake at last.
To be chosen to do God's work on earth,
To help those in need,
To feel a part of everything
Is a wonderful gift indeed.
To advance through every lifetime,
To see God's shining light each day,
And to finally hear those words at last:
"In my kingdom, my child, now you may stay."

Of Mice and Men

Early one Christmas, a long time ago,
I heard a tap tapping on my front door.
When I looked, there was no one around
Except for a mouse that made hardly a sound.

Then the mouse started singing a carol so sweet
While ringing some bells that were attached to his feet,
And when he had finished, he said with a smile,
"May I come in and stay for a while?"

Well, I thought, *it is Christmas*. So I said all right,
And the mouse came in, and he stayed the night.
He told me a story as we sat by the fire.
He assured me it was true and that he wasn't a liar.

He said God loves all life, even mice and men,
And he said one day we would both meet again.
He said, "Every creature has its purpose, you see.
Yes, even someone as small as me.

"And when we can learn to love all God's creations,
Respecting all species, colors, creeds, or nations,
That's when we become all we can be,
And this will apply to you and to me."

We talked all night until I fell fast asleep,
And I slept so well, with no need to count sheep.
It was the first restful night I'd had for so long,
And I dreamed of the mouse and his funny little song.

I awoke the next morning and my friend had gone,
But he'd left me so much to think upon.
I now understand that you can learn from everyone you meet,
Even a mouse with bells on his feet.

What Is Grief?

Looking back on my life to those days just before the darkness fell,
Grief was simply a word that others had told me felt like hell.
I suddenly lost my darling wife after many years of intolerable pain.
Then I came to know the sheer terror of grief, over and over again.

Now I've thought a lot about this word during my solitude, my time alone,
And ever since that day my loved one died, grief has cut me to the bone.
After thinking and talking about it, I now understand more these days
That everyone's grief is unique; and that we all react in different ways.

I understand the emotions I felt, though I still feel much regret.
So I've written these feelings down because I never want to forget
And I would like to help someone else who may be traveling the very same path
To come to terms with his or her grieving and to lesson any anger or wrath.

I experienced the physical pains of grief. The blinding headaches they came first,
Followed by pains in my chest. I thought my heart and lungs would burst.
Then came the mental anguish caused by grief, that feeling called despair.
I cried myself to sleep each night because you were no longer there.

With the anger left by grief, my spite for God was sown.
And why did you go without me? Why leave me on my own?
Then there was the guilt. That feeling was so strong.
Did I tell you that I loved you enough? What else did I do wrong?

Then there was the loneliness. That feeling hurt me the most,
The feeling that I could no longer go on, haunted by your ghost.
But now the anger and guilt are gone, and so are the physical pains.
The mental anguish has eased a lot, but the loneliness still remains.

And as long as this heart still beats and this mind remains intact,
Then grief will never completely die until my final act.
By then grief will be just a memory, which will finally come to an end
When I take my final journey to be with my wife, who was also my best friend.

The Breath of Love

The breath of love is sweet
Like honey on the tongue.
If only you could have realized this
When you were foolish and young,
Wasting time chasing lust,
Your hormones raging wild,
Bringing new life into this world
When you were but a child.
You thought you were making love,
But it was only lust.
So many young lives are ruined this way,
When love lies in the dust.
Did you stand beside her?
Or did you run away?
Did you brag about it to your friends?
If you did, one day you'll pay.
So now you think you're a man,
But you're still just one of the boys.
Respect is a word you don't understand.
You might as well still be playing with toys.
You know sex without love is worthless,
And there is nothing that can compare
With the sweet breath of love
And the smell of your loved one's hair.
I hope you will finally understand
And will maybe become a man one day.
And I hope you'll regret what you did to her,
But even if you do, there's a price to pay.
We are all responsible for our own actions,
Even when we are young,
So don't sour the breath of love that's sweet
Like honey on the tongue.

Farewell to the Flesh

I'm a spirit being a long way from home,
An alien in a foreign land.
But this is where I must be,
So this is where I make my stand.
I hide within this flesh,
Surrounded by sinew, skin, and bone.
It's just a vehicle for transport
For my soul, a temporal home.
I've been here for quite a while,
Because I've needed to pay my dues.
We each must go through many difficult things,
And some you win while others you lose.
I came here to learn in this earthly life,
And in this shell, I must be.
My higher self lies hidden inside,
So, what you see is not really me.
But I've finally realized who I am.
My higher self is taking command.
This was always meant to happen one day.
This is how it was always planned.
I can never go back to the person I was.
My eyes are now open, so there's no retreat,
And because of the harsh lessons I've learned,
If victory comes, it will be so sweet.
Only time will tell, of course,
But I'm determined to finish what I started
Before taking my leave from this earthly life
As one of the dearly departed.
That's just a way of saying I'm going home
To where my loved ones wait for me.
Then my spirit will say farewell to this flesh,
And my soul will finally be free.

Gareth W. Phillips

I Can Fly*

I didn't know it would be like this. I can fly. Oh my God, I can fly.
I haven't got wings, but I don't need them, for as spirit I can soar in the sky.
To think I was scared of dying, so scared of passing away.
Now I can fly like an eagle, far beyond our Milky Way.
I can travel beyond this universe, for I no longer need to breathe air.
There is nothing beyond my reach anymore; I only need to think and I'm there.
But if only you were here, too, to see the wonders I've seen,
Places no human being could survive, but that's exactly where I've been.

I've been to planets unknown here on earth and have traveled near and far.
I've seen every constellation and witnessed the birth of a star.
But despite all the wonders of the cosmos, I will always return to your side.
You see, love is God's greatest creation, and ours will never be denied.
But it doesn't matter where I am; think of me, and I'll be there.
For it only takes a second, and I'll be touching your face or your hair.
And the only time I'm ever sad is when I see you cry,
So please don't be unhappy, my love. Remember, we cannot die.

One day we will fly together, for there is so much I want you to see,
And I will never be completely satisfied until you are here with me.
But you still have much more to learn until we're together again,
So take a deep breath and carry on, and try to smile through the pain.
Remember your spirit cannot be harmed; immortal beings can never die.
We will never turn to dust, you know. That's just another lie.
And love will always endure, so just be patient and see this through.
Try to remember the good times, my love, and you know I'll be waiting for you.

This poem was given to me by my wife Tina in spirit in reply to the previous poem, which I had written the day before.

CHAPTER 7

A Higher Being

My Child

During the second half of 2012, I received several messages from a higher being who called me his child, so I often asked spirit to tell me who would call me his child. In the back of my mind, I thought this could be God, but then I thought, *Why would my God speak to me?* Then, on August 21 of that year, I received a message while I was in an altered state:

> A writer to my question God.

This message was obviously cryptic. (This is often the way they give messages to me.) I looked at it a couple of times and then left it so I could come back to it with a fresh mind. The next day I received a message from a medium in the Aberdare Spiritualist Church, and I understood the entire message except one thing. The medium told me she could see an old-fashioned wind-up gramophone with a horn attachment, and she asked me, "Is this a memory from your past?" I said I didn't think so.

The very next day, my friend Madeline asked me to go to B&Q with her to buy a hover mower. Afterward we went for a cup of tea, and I told her about the messages from a higher being who I thought could be God. Madeline laughed at this and said, "You're imagining things, Gareth." So, a little embarrassed, I quickly changed the subject and told her about the message I had received about the gramophone. Straight away Madeline said, "Oh, like the one with the little dog on the front, *His Master's Voice?*"

There was a stunned silence for a few seconds before Madeline said, "But it can't be God, Gareth. Why would he talk to you?" And I said, "That's the very same question I've been asking myself." When I arrived home later that day, I decided to look at the cryptic message again. Suddenly it all made sense. "A writer to my question God" became "You were asking the question who was the writer of the message. The answer is God."

I knew Tina was there, so I asked her if this was true. Then suddenly it became freezing cold and the room filled with a mist that was full of little glowing things that flew around and touched me all over, for me this is always means yes. So I am now certain that some of these messages are from God.

Then later, after it had all ended, I was feeling a little shocked, so I decided to ask another question: "Father, why me?" I immediately heard a loud but gentle voice saying, "Why not?"

The Book of Eli

The very next day I received a message from Hayley in our circle. This message came from my grandfather Thomas, who I know to be one of my helpers. He asked Hayley to tell me to find a book called *The Book of Eli*. This is not the book of the film bearing the same name and starring Denzel Washington but rather a completely different story written by someone called Sam Moffi. Later I purchased the book from Amazon.com, and it turned out to be the story of a man who crosses over to the other side and meets and is enlightened by many famous people who now reside there. He also meets Jesus, and he hears the voice of God.

He is then told that he will be sent back to his earthly life to teach others about the true word of God. He is told that he has tasks to perform for God and the world of spirit. At the end of the book, he is sent back to the earth a changed man, and with the knowledge he has acquired, he begins the work as he had promised.

After reading this book, I realized that earlier messages I had received from my grandfather about becoming a spiritual teacher were now being reinforced by the message he had given me through Hayley. This is how my grandfather seems to work with me: he gives me a message, which I write down, and then at a later date, I receive a message from a medium in a church or in the circle that confirms what he has already told me.

This is the proof he knows I need to let me know that I'm not imagining things. The strange thing is that I also left my body and was taken into the spirit world by my wife Tina several months after she had passed to spirit. I know I was only allowed to remember some of the things that happened during my visit. But I also have this nagging feeling that there was much more I was not allowed to remember at that time. And, very much like the character's experience in the book, the visit I had to the spirit world changed me forever. Since that visit, I have become far more aware of the true nature of our earthly visits and why I am here now. And I know with great certainty that I am becoming more and more like my higher self with each passing day.

I have no idea where or to what this is going to lead me to, but I have very strong feelings of excitement, anticipation, and impatience to be getting on with what I am meant to do.

Oh and by the way, on the cover of *The Book of Eli*, it shows Eli talking to God and saying, "Why me?" to which God then replies, "Why not?"— the very same question I asked and the very same reply I received.

Talking to God

I mentioned earlier in the book my problems with my family after Tina's death, but I also had problems finding a job. At this point, I was feeling desperate, and my family's problems seemed to be getting worse, not better. I was trying to live on seventy pounds a week and run a car that I needed to take my family members to hospital and doctor appointments, so I had very little money for food. I found myself at the mercy of a government that was about to inflict upon me, and many others, the so-called bedroom tax. When Tina was alive, we had been moved into a flat with an extra bedroom because I was looking after my wife, who needed a hospital bed and a hoist. But now that she had passed away, I felt like I was being taxed for losing her. It was no wonder I felt depressed.

As I said earlier, I still hadn't found work. After applying for more than two hundred jobs and only having five interviews, I was beginning to lose all hope because there were so many other people out there after those same jobs. I was also now sixty years old. I felt like I didn't have a hope in hell. I became very depressed. I expected help from the job center to locate work, but all I got was pressure to apply for a certain amount of jobs every week. Of course, the illness in my family didn't exactly help matters. And even though my wife Tina had been gone for several years at that point, I still felt the pain of her loss. While at home, I often talked to God and my loved ones in spirit.

One day in February 2013, because I felt so desperate and so alone, I found myself saying aloud, "Father, why am I being punished? I must have done something terrible in a previous life to deserve this." Suddenly, I heard a deep voice saying, "Gareth, you are not being punished. You have done nothing wrong." I had to wait for around nine weeks before it was explained to me in full. Now I understand, but it's still just as painful.

A Message from a Higher Being

On the day before my sixty-first birthday, while meditating I heard the question, "Almighty God, why hast thou forsaken me?" There was a slight pause and then I heard the following words:

> I have not forsaken you, Gareth. I will never forsake you, my son. We are connected by love, you and I, as all my children are connected to me. You, Gareth, have been sent to this earth to do my bidding, and you will do this, my son, you will. There will be no stone left unturned in the help you will be given, and the information and knowledge we will impart to you will make a huge difference in the new life you are going to lead. Believe me, Gareth, the best is yet to come, and you will open so many eyes and hearts to the true meaning of love.

> Gareth, the road you have travelled has been extremely hard, and you of all people should know why it has had to be this way. If you don't walk the walk yourself, how can you help others put one foot in front of the other? You

needed to sample all the harsh things you went through to shape you into the being you are today.

Gareth, you should be proud of the way you have stood up to every single challenge thrown at you. We are all proud of you. I can see your light shining now. Your light will always shine for those who need it the most.

Gareth, I know your heart is good, and I know you are far stronger than you give yourself credit for. So tighten your belt, throw back your shoulders, stick out your chest, and hold your head up high because you deserve to be heard, Gareth, and you will be heard.

CHAPTER 8

Yet More Poems

A Better World

Let's pray for a world without anger
And a world free from shame.
Imagine a world with equality,
Where everyone is treated the same.
Pray for a world without envy
And a world without any greed.
Imagine a world where all people are content
And will only take what they need.
Pray for a world without bitterness
And a world free from spite.
Imagine a world that thrives on compassion,
Where everyone has seen the light.
Pray for a world where one hungry person
Would cause everyone to shed a tear,
Where no one could die of starvation
And no one would have any fear.
Think about a world without conflict,
Because there'd simply be no one to hate.
Imagine a world full of sisters and brothers.
Let's pray that it isn't too late.
Pray for a world full of joy
And a world full of respect,

Where no one need sleep in a cardboard box
Or could die of sheer neglect.
Think about a world where we live as one,
Despite color, creed, or nation.
Pray for a world where animals are safe
From laboratory experimentation.

Imagine a world where wild animals roam free
And are never kept in cages.
Pray for a world where children don't work
In sweatshops for pitiful wages.
Imagine a world with total peace,
Where no one carries a gun,
A world where children would still be safe
Out of sight of their parents and having fun.
Imagine a world without refugees
Having to flee across borders
Because of some despot who thinks he's a god
And is born to give everyone orders.
Imagine a world without different religions,
Where one God would be proclaimed.
Pray for a world without hatred,
Where no one is tortured or maimed.
Pray for a world with understanding,
Where love isn't replaced by the fist,
Where there are no religious zealots
And suicide bombers could never exist.
Pray for a world full of caring
And then imagine a world brand new,
Where no one is ashamed of his or her feelings
And love comes shining through,
A world where we show love freely,
Where men are not scared of emotion,
A world where love can cross all boundaries
And sail across every ocean.
I'd love to live in a world like this,

Where greed and hate can have no place,
Where no one has heard of blue blood,
And there is no superior race,
A world where no one feels inferior,
Where everyone is agreeing,
Where no one will be able to look down his or her nose
At another human being.

I'm Not a Hypochondriac

I hear there's a virus going around; I hope I don't catch it.
I've got a boil somewhere nasty, and I've been told I shouldn't scratch it.
Spondylitis plays hell with my back, my shoulders, and my neck.
Arthritis affects most of my joints. I really am a wreck

I'm allergic to anti-inflammatory drugs, so they don't help at all.
I've got irritable bowel syndrome, and that drives me up the wall.
I don't sleep very well at night because my arms go quite numb.
I've got hemorrhoids like marbles and a pimple on my bum.

I suffer with neuralgia and sinus trouble as well.
I get ringing in my ears that sounds just like a bell.
I've had asthma as well as vertigo; I've had fluid on the knee
And an elbow that locks quite often. I think someone is picking on me.

I've had an ingrown toenail, and I've got a bunion as well.
At least I haven't got BO. Hang on, what's that smell?
I've had cameras in every orifice, even one up my nose.
I won't tell you where the others went, but you'll guess, I suppose.

Carpel tunnel in both wrists, athlete's foot from borrowed shoes,
And a tonsil that grew back—it's no wonder I've got the blues.
I suffer with sore throats, and my jaw locks now and again.
I'm told that's just arthritis, and I must put up with the pain.

So apart from that I'm okay. I really am doing quite well.

But why did you ask to see me, Doctor? Oh my God, I've got that as well?
Look, I'm not a hypochondriac, but I have written out my will,
And I've asked for these words to be put on my headstone: I told you I
was ill.

A Simple Life

Live your life as simply as you can.
You must realize by now that you're more than a man
And lusting for power is the way of the fool.
So listen to spirit. That's the first rule.

Diamonds and gold have no real worth.
You will find more pleasure from Mother Earth,
For your soul is evolving while you live,
So be open to receive as well as to give.

Lust is for fools, so seek only love.
Put your faith in God and heaven above.
Look to the light. Ignore all that's dark.
Find the being inside and follow that spark.

Don't carry the burden of anger and hate.
Live a simple life, for it's never too late.
Forget the past and a future day.
Live in the present, for this is the way.

Come join the party. Don't sit by yourself.
Enjoy God's blessings; they're much better than wealth.
Bring love to the forefront in all that you do,
For a heart that's pure is a heart that's true.

Take most of your pleasure from things that don't cost,
For the way of true happiness has almost been lost.
These simple truths I now give to you.
So now, my child, you should know what to do.

A Ship of Fools

I sailed upon the ship of fools
And followed other people's rules
Until the day I began to see
That the biggest fool onboard was me.
When we're dead, we're dead, and we turn to dust.
That rubbish I was told I used to trust.
They tell you a lie that you will believe.
They tell you when you're young and naïve
About death and hell that doesn't exist
To frighten you, and they will persist.
But now I know the reason why
We don't just live and wait to die.
Eternal life we must embrace
On earth and then in a better place
Because heaven's light will welcome us all,
Old and young, big and small.
So there's no such thing as an endless night
Because we live again when we enter the light.
Nothing ends at the body's demise
Because we live forever. No one dies.
The decaying body will feed the earth
While we go forward to another rebirth.
Our path is long, and it has no end,
And love is the only way, my friend.
Now the ship of fools has sunk without a trace,
And I can serve my God with a smile on my face.

It's Raining Again

In Wales we get a lot of rain.
Sometimes the weather's obscene.
But we need a drop of water.
It keeps our country green.
And it's very cold right now.

There's lots of hail and sleet.
And with all this rain we're having,
We should really have webbed feet.

There was a slug on my carpet this morning.
He'd come in out of the rain.
So I gently moved him to one side.
I couldn't evict him again.
I've never seen so much water.
Who knows when it's going to end?
But in a couple of months, we might have a drought,
And they'll say on the telly to bathe with a friend.

Well, I'm quite open to that idea
If I can find someone to share.
But I've got a shower instead of a bath,
So I'll have to look elsewhere.
But that could be in the future.
At the moment, the rain's still falling.
It looks like I'm going to be stuck indoors
Because this weather is really appalling.

It's enough to make a frog swear.
It's enough to make a duck curse.
And this is the Welsh summer.
The winter is bound to be worse.

Respect

We have billions of brothers and sisters, most of them we'll never see.
But we are all part of one family, and that's how it was meant it to be.

Not a minute goes by each day without the tears of a mother
Because someone has taken her son's life, someone has killed a spiritual brother.

We don't respect life as much as we did; in fact, it's become dirt cheap.
There's death and destruction all over this world, and we hardly lose any sleep.

We've become so used to the violence that we hardly shed a tear,
Unless it's someone we actually know, like family or someone dear.

It's shoved in our faces all the time; it's on the national news every day.
It's the damning proof of our inhuman nature; we are surrounded by moral decay.

And we have little respect for the animal kingdom; we treat them with disdain.
Extinction may be their future, and all they expect from us is pain.

We have lost our spiritual birthright, which we were given at the start.
We have turned away from the path. There is nothing but greed in man's heart.

There was a time when it wasn't like this; man hunted when there was a need.
He only took what he had to, because he had a family to feed.

But now man kills for sport. He kills for greed and hate.
No matter if the blood is animal or human, they all share a similar fate.

And the longer we have lived on this earth, the less human we've become.
Man now kills without regret. There is no conscience. Man's heart is numb.

Our spiritual heritage is disappearing; we treat all living things with neglect.
So is there any hope for the human race, which has little if any respect?

When I Dream

When I dream I go to a wondrous place
Where I'm with lost loved ones again.
Smiling faces all around,
With no sign of grief or pain.
Oh, how I love to dream,
To leave my body at rest,
To see my life as it really is
And not be so distressed.
In dreams I find the truth.
In dreams I'm finally free.
I'm a citizen of the universe,
And there's a spark of God in me.
I have come to know that I'm never alone.
I've become one with everything.
I'm not merely a human being;
I have his spark, so I'm part of him.
And it only happens when I dream,
When everything becomes so clear.
I know we are all from the same source,
So we should never have any fear.
One day I'll leave this body behind.
I won't need it anymore.
So please don't shed a tear for me.
I'll be very happy to go.
There will be nothing to be sad about.
All my troubles I'll leave in my wake.
I'll be going back home with a smile on my face
On that final journey I take.

A Cry for Help

This is a cry for help from above.
Please teach us, Lord, that it's all about love.
It's not about power, and it's not about greed.

73

These are negative things that we don't need.
Love is the cure for every problem,
And it has the solution that's needed to solve them.
Fear is the enemy that halts our progression,
But love is the answer to every question.

Love's at the center of everyone's core,
So we only need to open the door.
It can never leave us, it's constant and true,
And it's inside waiting to be freed by you.
But so many today seem satisfied with lust,
Though it sours our lives and can turn them to dust.
The human ego takes much of the blame
Because we think we are separate, but we're all the same.

We are each a part of one great life-form,
And in the spirit world this is the norm.
We were sent from the source to learn and progress,
To discover our divinity, to become more, never less.
We are part of the power that created heaven and earth,
And that power is responsible for giving us birth.
Unconditional love is what we strive to attain.
That's why we keep coming back time and again.

So open your heart and free your mind.
The truth is out there for all to find.
It's a four-letter word that comes from above.
It's simple. It's easy. The word is love.

Sunshine in the Morning

Sunshine in the morning,
The smell of hot buttered toast,
The birds that sing outside your home,
A kiss from the one you love the most.
The flowers in your garden,

The butterflies and the bees,
Having the time to read a good book
Or do whatever you please.
A cool breeze in the summer,
The first signs of spring,
Autumnal colors on the trees,
And hearing a choir sing.
Watching your children sleeping,
Nursing them when they cry,
Hearing them say I love you
And knowing that isn't a lie.
A drink down the pub with Dad,
The sound of Mother's voice,
The unconditional love of a pet,
Or just being with a friend of your choice.
Sitting beside a river,
Listening to the song it sings,
A gentle melodic lullaby,
Is definitely one of my favorite things.
The gentle touch of your beloved
And little ones at play,
Just some of the things we take for granted
Each and every single day.

Thank You

Thank you, Father, for giving me life
And for the moon and stars in the sky.
Thank you for the lessons I've had to learn
And for letting me know that we cannot die.
Thank you for the sun that shines every day,
Even though it isn't always seen.
Thank you for the clouds that bring the rain
That makes this land so green.
Thank you for all four seasons
And many thanks for the birds and the bees.

Thank you for the flowers and the plants
And oxygen from the trees.
Thank you for the laughter of children
And thank you for a mother's kiss.
Thank you for the grandparents who spoiled us
And who we very often miss.
And I'd personally like to thank you, Father,
For my dad, who taught me respect,
For my mother, who often went without
And never showed any neglect.
Thank you for the joy of Christmas
And for the toys from Santa's sack,
And for thirty-four years with the woman I loved
And for the love that she gave me back.
Thank you for everyone who helped me
After all the tears that were cried.
Thank for showing me the way to this church
And for all the friends who meet inside.
In fact, thank you for all my family and friends
And for the pets that gave me their love.
I know I have so much to be grateful for,
So, Father, thank you for all the above.

That Nagging Feeling

Are you satisfied with your life, or do you feel like you're falling short?
Do you feel as though something is missing? Have all your dreams come
to naught?
Is there a nagging feeling deep inside telling you something is wrong?
Then you still have time to change your life. This is not the end of your
song.

Spirit is trying to guide you to where you obviously need to be.
And until you find your purpose in life, from these feelings you won't be
free.

It's that nagging thought that keeps returning, that something isn't quite right,
That sensation that won't go away, the one keeping you awake at night.

Sometimes we fall short of our dreams, never climbing to the heights to which we aspire,
Maybe through a lack of assurance or maybe someone has put out our fire.
Sometimes others will put us down, and we believe whatever they say,
But you must listen to the voice in your head that will never go away.

Sometimes we're around the wrong people and constantly feeling annoyed,
But we're scared to move away because our confidence has been destroyed.
But spirit is always there to inspire you, and all you need to do is believe.
Your loved ones are still beside you, and they will never ever leave.

But if you do fall short in this life, you will have to repeat your mistakes.
But you really can do it now, and having more confidence is all it takes.
Don't listen to all the doubters. Never let them inside your head.
Your loved ones in spirit are already there, so just listen to them instead.

Your connection can not be severed, and eventually you'll become aware
That your loved ones are trying to guide you and that they will always be there.

The Watcher

There is no death, the watcher said. It's a false belief inside your head.
Reality is always hidden from our view, and you never see the real you
Until awareness opens your eyes and frees you then from earthly lies.

There is no time, the watcher said. It doesn't exist, and the dead are not dead.
Time's an illusion for those on earth, a dream of life that follows rebirth.
All reality is hidden from your eyes, so you live this life in a human disguise.

The real you is inside, the watcher said, and through life's experience your soul is fed.

A belief in death is a terrible blow, but grief will be easier for those who know.

We watch you grieve and we watch you cry until you find out that spirit can't die.

You don't always sleep, the watcher said. Your soul will travel when your body's in bed.

You can visit loved ones, you can see them all, though very rarely you will recall

Only when there's an absolute need. Then your memory can be freed.

When it's your time, the watcher said, the truth will be known, the darkness shed.

From whence you came, you will return, with all the lessons you were meant to learn,

To be with your loved ones, safe at last, all lives then remembered from your past.

For I am the watcher. I see it all. I watch you climb, and I see you fall.

I tell you now you will not burn, for there is no hell. This too you will learn.

I am the father. You are daughter and son. And through my love, your life was begun.

Sisters and brothers, side by side, all my children with me will abide.

You need not believe to receive my love; you will still be welcomed into heaven above.

I am the watcher, I'm always there, I am the father, and I will always care.

His Heavenly Throne

Every house is a house of God
As long as there's love inside.
Every home is a sanctuary
When God is allowed to abide.

Don't leave him outside your door.
Welcome the Lord and ask him to stay.
And never deny his existence,
For this is the spiritual way.

If he is in your heart,
You can never be alone.
Know that God is the master of all
Who sits on his heavenly throne.

We are all the children of God,
Even when you refuse to believe.
But once you bid him enter your heart,
Then he will never leave.

His heavenly kingdom awaits us,
Where contentment and peace will be found,
Where we can never again hurt another
Because there only love will abound.

One day we will all find the truth.
It will be there for everyone to see.
For the thing we call death will be a blessing
When another human soul will rejoice and be free.

CHAPTER 9

Another Pathway

Shutting Down

Most people who work for spirit learn to shut down after working or meditating, but I never used to do this, which (unbeknown to me) was the reason I was always so tired. One day I learned why I needed to shut down after working. I was sitting at the back of our church, feeling totally drained. I felt so weak that I could hardly stand up to sing the hymns with the rest of the congregation. That's when a local medium sat next to me and explained why I was so tired. He told me that I was surrounded by spirit beings and many of them were firemen who had lost their lives in the 9-11 disaster.

The medium's name was Ray Pugh, and he told me that the reason they were with me all the time and were draining my energy was because I was constantly open to spirit by not shutting down. Because of this, they were able to see my light and were looking to me for help. Ray told me to speak to them and help them to go into the light, which is what I did. I told them to enter the light and that they would still be able to see their earthbound loved ones and meet up with other loved ones who had already passed into spirit. I was shocked at what happened next: I felt a huge weight being lifted off me, and I felt as light as a feather. My energy instantly returned, and I felt quite normal again.

Ray informed me that he had seen these spirit beings with me when he had taken the service in our church several days earlier and said that he had come to our church again on this day to help me.

When I got home, a thought came to me. I was sure I had written and drawn things in a book I used to keep for recording everything I saw or heard while meditating. There were entries that I thought were about disasters that were to come in the future, because I had been showed future events previously. But when I looked through the pages, I found that I had been drawing firemen with breathing apparatuses and lamps on their helmets, I had drawn buildings falling, and I had heard people shouting and screaming.

I had also written about an earthquake I thought was going to happen in San Fernando in the future. I saw buildings falling down a mountainside and heard an old song called "Last Train to San Fernando."

At that time, I had thought that everything I was given was going to happen in the future, but now I know differently; I was being contacted because these lost souls needed my help, but unfortunately, I couldn't see them. Thank God for Ray, who had worked as a rescue medium in the past and new exactly what to do. This also brought back an earlier memory for me that also involved the rescue of a lost soul. I had just moved into a flat with my wife Tina, who was quite ill. I knew there was a presence in the flat before we moved in, and I knew it was an elderly lady. This lady played tricks on me by moving objects around, but for some reason she didn't like my wife being there and had frightened her on several occasions.

This was at least five years before I became a spiritualist, but somehow I knew exactly what to do. I told her that she was not supposed to be there and that she was lost. I told her that if she entered the light, all would be well.

She had been with us for a few months at that time, but after I said those words, I didn't hear from her again until around eight years later when I received a message from a medium called Sheryl Jones, who told me that there was an elderly lady with her who wished to thank me for helping her into the light so that she could return home. Thinking about this now, I realize that this episode with the elderly lady was the beginning of me becoming aware of spirit again.

A New Path

When I first joined the circle at the Aberdare Spiritualist Church in 2008, there were about twelve of us, but over time it dwindled to just three people. Hayley Evans led the circle, and the other person in our little group was Pauline Williams, who I have known for about thirty years. The three of us have become good friends, and we all look forward to the time we can spend with each other and spirit.

At the time that I wrote this, it seemed that spirit thought we needed to do something different, because Hayley was told that we needed to take our circle outdoors.

Now my grandfather Thomas, who is a regular spirit visitor to our circle, told Hayley that the place we needed to go was on top of a mountain, near a waterfall. I thought for a while, and then I remembered the place he was talking about. I often used to go there to meditate. The place was at the top of the Rhigos Mountain Road, overlooking Hirwaun Common, and was on the way to the valley town of Treherbert. This was only a few hundred meters from one of my favorite places, Craig-y-Llyn. So we decided to take our little circle outdoors as soon as we were able, to the place my grandfather had described. And at the end of our meeting, I heard someone say to me, "For what we are about to receive, may the Lord make us truly thankful."

The following week at 10:00 a.m., we set out on our short journey to the place that spirit wanted us to be. Across the road from this place is what's left of an old Iron Age settlement. The remains can still be seen quite clearly when you get close to them. But when we arrived at the picnic spot nearby, we couldn't see much because of the dense fog. When we got out of the car, Pauline said, "Why, I'm being drawn toward the woods behind us." Hayley replied, "We do need to enter these woods." So we did.

And as we entered the woods, I began to feel very cold, much colder than I had felt in the parking area. Pauline wandered away from us and seemed to become frozen to the spot near a tree stump, and she was looking up at the sky. That's when I heard someone say, "It's the way to the stars."

Then suddenly everything really kicked off. Hayley said, "Oh my God, Gareth, can you feel that?" Suddenly, I shuddered. It felt as if something or someone had passed right through my body. Hayley said, "They're all running toward us." Every time one of these souls passed by or through us, we both shuddered. I have never felt cold like that in my life; it didn't feel natural at all.

Hayley was then told that we needed to move forward into a clearing just ahead of us. That's when everything got even colder and even more unwelcoming.

The next thing I knew, I was hearing spirit voices louder than I had ever heard them before: "Go away from this place; you are not welcome." Hayley was getting the same messages, while Pauline was still frozen next to the tree stump. As we looked across at her, she said she saw a woman tied to a stake and that this woman was looking up to the heavens, praying. I then heard someone say, "They were cannibals." I told Hayley this, and she said, "Yes, they were," so she had obviously heard the same thing. Then she heard someone say, "You'd better go now because Jason is coming."

We left the woods, not because we were told to go and were frightened, but because Hayley had been told that we needed to visit another place. We all knew that very bad things had happened there and that many poor souls had lost their lives. But even though the things we were hearing, seeing, and feeling were very dark, we didn't feel in any danger at all. I think we all knew that we were being protected.

As we left the woods, Hayley heard someone say, "You are now on a new pathway." Our next destination was the car park near Craig-y-Llyn itself, which is the highest point in the South Wales Valleys. Almost as soon as we got out of the car, we knew we weren't welcome here either, because we all heard more voices telling us to go away.

At this local beauty spot, there is usually a van selling food, drinks, and ice cream, so while my two companions went for a cup of tea, I went down the small incline near the picnic tables to a spot where some locals scatter the ashes of their departed loved ones. As I approached the area where all the crosses of lost loved ones were scattered around, I was again told, "Go away. You are not welcome here," but I didn't take any notice of this. It was then that I heard someone else say, "Welcome back, my son. It's the graveyard next." I joined the others and told them what I had heard. That's when Hayley was told of a place on the mountain where many bodies had been buried a very long time ago.

So we set off again, back in the direction of the Treherbert side of the mountain. Only a few hundred meters past the spot at which we had stopped first, Hayley said, "Turn here." I turned the car, and we found ourselves on a rough forestry road lined with trees on both sides. About a hundred meters up the track, we stopped and got out of the car. We only had to wait a few minutes before we saw a spirit in the woods on the other side of the road.

He kept peering around a tree every now and again, and then I heard someone say the name Rodger and then "Rodger the dodger," which made us all laugh. Hayley said he was harmless, and then suddenly, he was gone. Then I heard someone say, "Stop laughing. Jason is coming." Pauline said she could hear them coming through the trees toward us, and then Hayley said, "Oh my God, look at this shit."

Hayley had seen a very ominous bank of thick fog rolling out from the woods and coming very rapidly toward us. Then we heard someone say, "It's the hunting party." That's when Hayley cried out in pain and said that it felt as if someone had struck her leg with a spear. Then, as abruptly as it had started, the fog stopped about ten meters away from us and seemed unable to come any closer. I heard someone say, "Stand your ground, for you are protected." It was a very strange sight, indeed, to see this bank of thick fog frozen in midair.

Whatever was in the woods on that side of the road didn't want us there, and they knew that we were aware of them. Then we all turned to look into the woods on the other side of the road, and Hayley said she could see people hiding there, afraid to come out. I then heard someone say, "Many are trapped between two worlds." That was when I realized why we were there: we had been sent there by spirit to help those lost and frightened souls to find their way home by entering God's light. I told the others this, and I began to pray and tell those lost souls to enter the light and that there they would find love, peace, and protection.

Hayley said that they were leaving the trees and coming toward us because the light was just behind us. Most of the beings entered the light, but some stayed behind. As the last stragglers entered the light, I heard someone say, "Thank you," and Hayley said that the last one who went through had kissed her cheek. We then heard someone say, "It's all over.

You have done God's work." Then slowly but surely the strange fog bank disappeared.

Hayley said, "I think I need a cigarette after that." As she lit her much-needed cigarette and blew the smoke out, something very strange happened. Instead of the smoke gradually dissipating into the air, it formed a solid shape that slowly and deliberately drifted past us. As we watched the shape drift by, we stared in total amazement. Then again, this was just another of the weird and incredible things that had happened to us that morning, so we really shouldn't have been surprised at all.

None of us had seen anything like it before. It was as if we were being given a sign from spirit. As we stood there, waiting to see if anything else was going to happen, we all heard a voice from spirit say, "Holy smoke." That's when I said to the others, "You know, I think that's my father-in-law, Trevor. I'm sure I can feel him here." Hayley then laughed and said Trevor, who is another regular visitor to our circle, had just owned up to it by saying, "You got me."

I believe that the entities on the other side of the road who had tried to attack us were responsible for the terrible things done at this remote place and that they were scared to enter the light, thinking that they would be punished. However, it was only a feeling, so I can't be sure.

Hayley had said earlier that she had been told that our pathway was changing. Now I heard the song, "Fool (If You Think It's Over)." I wasn't sure what this meant, but I thought we were either being told that we would be doing this sort of work again in other places or that we need to come back to this place because we had more work to do here.

After our little adventure came to an end, Hayley asked me to take a couple photos of her and Pauline. In all the time I've known Pauline and Hayley, I've never seen them so animated and happy. I felt a similar euphoria myself. It felt as if we had done something incredibly important, and I couldn't stop smiling. As we were leaving, I heard someone say again, "You have been doing God's work."

What we did that day is known in spiritualist circles as rescue mediumship or spirit rescue. I'd had some experience with this in the past and had previously asked a medium friend of mine if this was something I might be doing in the future, but all he said was that he wasn't sure and that I would just have to wait and see. Well, now I knew, and it looked as if this was our new pathway. However, I obviously couldn't do this on my own because I don't see spirit as clearly as Hayley does. Spirit seems to have created a little team to work together, and between the three of us, we have all the tools we need to do this sort of work. I truly believe that we are doing God's work.

What a morning that was. I didn't know about the others, but I couldn't wait for our next adventure. Bring it on, I thought! And I am very grateful for what we received that day.

Well, we didn't have to wait long for our next adventure and to find out what "Fool If You Think It's Over" meant. Now, when I talk about hearing a song, this is one of the ways I get messages from my lovely Tina in spirit. I will cover this subject a little later in the book.

A Guest in My Home

A few days after our experience on the mountain, I started to smell woodsmoke in my spare bedroom—and only in my spare bedroom. This went on for about a week. I instinctively knew that I had brought a spirit being home with me. I felt the presence of a young girl in my flat, and every time I meditated, I kept seeing the spot we had recently visited on the mountain. I also had several dreams about what we had done there. Later, while meditating with a friend, We kept hearing the name Timmy.

So a few days later in the circle, I suggested to Hayley that we needed to make another trip to Craig-y-Llyn because this spirit had now become attached to me. When I told her about needing to return, she suddenly asked me if I knew someone called Timmy. I told her that I had been hearing that name over and over since our adventure and that it was probably from my young guest.

So we decided that we needed to return. By this time, we were no longer a group of three but four; our close friend Marie had joined our little group. A few days later, we set off again to the place where we'd had our most incredible spiritual experience. There wasn't any fog this time, and there wasn't such an eerie feeling either, but it was very, very cold and windy.

The last time we were there, Hayley had said there were still some spirits who had not entered the light. I thought there was probably a connection between the young girl and Timmy, who had likely both stayed behind.

As soon as we got to the exact same spot as last time, Hayley saw someone watching us from the woods. We stood together facing that side of the wood, and as we had previously agreed, I began to say a prayer and asked Timmy and the young girl, who by now we realized was his older sister, to enter the light. But they didn't move and refused to enter. Just then, Hayley turned to me and said, "Who is Mary?" Well, we didn't have to wait very long to find out. When Mary arrived about thirty seconds later, the two children stepped forward and entered the light to be with her. They were gone in an instant.

It's at times like these that I wish I could still see spirit, but it doesn't happen to me often now. These days I seem to be clairaudient and clairsentient only, which is quite irritating to me after what I was able to see in the past. I hope the clairvoyance will return one day, but only time will tell.

We have come to believe that Mary was the mother of the two children who had become trapped between the two worlds. Who knows how long they had been searching for her before we became involved. I do know that the young girl, whose name I never found out, came back to visit me a few times over the next year or so. I know that because each time she came back, I could smell woodsmoke and feel her presence. I guess she was just trying to say thank you, but there was no real need because doing this sort of work brings its own rewards.

Aberfan

Since the end of July 2014, I had been told by spirit that our little group needed to visit the Aberfan cemetery, where many young children who had died in a disaster were buried. However, this was obviously going to be painful for Hayley, who had lost her son, Lewis, at a very young age. So when she didn't respond, I let it slide. But when our circle broke up for the school holidays, we were at a loss for something to keep us going, and then Hayley suffered a heart attack. So several weeks later, Pauline, Marie, and I decided to take a trip to Aberfan in late October.

Our trip occurred about forty-eight years after a tragic disaster had claimed the lives of twenty-eight adults and 116 very young children when an old coal tip had slid down the mountain after torrential rain. It completely engulfed a school and devastated the little valley community. I knew where Aberfan was, but I didn't know where the cemetery was located, so we kept a sharp look out for it as we drove. Suddenly Marie, who was in the rear of the car, told us that a little boy had just grabbed her hand, and as this happened, we saw the cemetery on the side of the mountain. We proceeded toward it and parked next to an old boarded-up church. We then made our way up the steep slope toward the graves of the victims of the Aberfan disaster.

It was quite early in the morning, and there was a bit of a nip in the air, but as we got closer to the graves, it seemed to get even colder. I then found myself saying, "Suffer the little children to come unto me."

This came as a bit of a shock at the time because I didn't have a clue why I said this out loud. As we walked alongside the white gravestones, we saw each of the twelve names that the three of us had been given a few days earlier. Marie stopped and said that the same little boy had grabbed her hand again, right next to a grave that contained two brothers. She then said it was the youngest boy who had grabbed her hand. We faced the graves and held hands as we said a prayer, and I asked all those who had not yet entered the light to do so.

After we did this, I heard someone say, "Bless you. Bless you. You are doing God's work." Then, as we moved around the last of the gravestones, we saw a statue of Jesus holding his hands out in front of him. Beneath the statue were the words, *Suffer the little children to come unto me*—the very words I had spoken as we neared the graves. I believe these children had gotten stuck between this world and the next because they could not bear to leave their parents. Forty-eight years later, their parents had probably all passed over to the other side themselves, and the souls of these children didn't know how to join them. That is why we were sent there.

I know some people will find this hard to believe, but it happened exactly the way I have described it. I know that there is even more work for us to do. Oh, and by the way, two days before this event, Marie and I had just started a relationship that I had been told by spirit three years earlier would last for the rest of our lives.

I have a very vivid memory of where I was on the morning of the Aberfan disaster. I was fourteen years old, and I had just broken my hand in school that very morning. Because it was only a few minute walk from my school to the Aberdare hospital, I was told by a teacher to make my own way there.

I waited for hours for someone to come and see to me. I seemed to be the only person in the hospital that morning. Finally, I saw a nurse, who sent me for an X-ray, and then I had to wait another hour or so to be put in plaster. I found out later that the reason for my long wait was that all the doctors and nurses were in Aberfan.

Over the next few weeks or so, word of the deaths of those poor children and adults appeared on the news every single day, and the story went worldwide. It, and where I was at the time, isn't something I will ever forget.

Spirit Rescue

I can't remember the date of our next little adventure, but it was near the end of 2014. One of Marie's nieces asked if we could get rid of a spirit that was frightening the children, so we agreed to try to help the spirit back into the light. The night before our trip, I had a dream. Well, it was more like a nightmare, really. I saw myself entering a house and climbing the stairs. At the top of the stairs, I turned to my right and entered a bedroom. I stood there for a few seconds before looking up at the ceiling. In the ceiling was a trap door to the attic that suddenly slid open, and a woman's face appeared. She had long dark hair and quite a thin face. She looked straight at me. Well, as you can probably guess, that woke me up with a bit of a start.

The following day, as we made our way to Abercwmboi without Hayley, who was still recovering from her heart attack, I told Marie and Pauline about my dream. When we arrived at the house, Marie's niece Lisa was waiting for us. She said the problem was in the bedroom on the right at the top of the stairs and that the children were being frightened by a woman who popped her head out of the door to the attic. We all looked at each other and laughed. Then we told Lisa about my dream.

When we were ready, we went up the stairs and entered the bedroom. As usual, we held hands, said our prayer, and then I told this lady to enter the light, where she would be cared for and be able to see all her loved ones in spirit once more.

At the time of this writing, it has been more than two years since the woman last appeared, so hopefully now she is where she is happy at last. I know that this is not the last time we will be doing this type of work, but for now we must all be patient and see what comes our way.

CHAPTER 10

Poems Again

Smile

Please dry your eyes.
You've shed enough tears for today.
You should have realized by now
That I haven't gone away.
And there's no need to feel ashamed.
Even the strongest will cry.
Your feelings do you credit.
Just remember, we don't die.

Death is just a rumour.
Everlasting life is a fact.
Our essence doesn't disappear,
So there is no final act.
Our energy lives forever,
And love will soldier on,
Getting stronger with every lifetime,
And to me you still belong.

What cannot speak cannot lie.
My thoughts you will come to understand.
I am with you for eternity,
Just as God had planned.

We two have always been one
And are only parted for a while.
But I'm still only a whisper away,
So come on now. Let's see you smile.

Metabolism

When I was young, I never got tired, and there weren't enough hours in the day.
I couldn't wait to get home from school, to get outdoors and play.
I was always so full of energy. I couldn't stop moving at all.
I drove my poor father mad. I drove him up and over the wall.

"Can't you keep still, boy? Have you got worms in you know where?
Or have you got ants in your pants? Bugger off out and get some fresh air."
I never could put any weight on. I burned it all off, you see.
And when I look at old photos, I can't believe that skinny kid is me.

It must have been a problem for my parents. It looked like I'd never been fed.
I could imagine the neighbors saying, "If they don't feed him soon, he'll be dead."
And I heard all those cruel jokes: "If he turns sideways he'll disappear.
There's more meat on a twig. Where's his bum? He's got no rear!"

I was given the nickname skinny dog, later in my teens,
For there was more meat on a whippet. I looked like Gandhi in a pair of jeans.
So I prayed, *Let me put weight on*, and at last God answered my prayer.
But did you have to overdo it, Father. You know this isn't fair.

I used to be able to eat anything, and I was always under twelve stone.
Now I'm scared to get on my scales in case I hear the bugger groan.
I think God has a wicked sense of humor, and I'm sure he's having a laugh.
I only need to look at a burger now, and I put on a stone and a half.

I'm told it's just my metabolism, and I'm a different shape today.
I'm told my bum's my best feature now. What a cruel thing to say.
Oh well, that's just the way it is. That's just the way it must be.
God has got a wicked sense of humor, but I know he's still smiling down
on me.

Sowing the Seeds of Love

Sow the seeds of love.
Plant them wherever you go.
Open your heart to the universe.
Then love in return you'll know.
Hate is a negative reaction.
It isn't needed at all.
So let go of all anger and jealousy.
Save yourself from that fall.
Discover the truth in love.
Be positive in all that you do.
Purify your soul
Because it's all about changing you.
Find the path of least resistance.
Let your life run smooth and clear.
Let obstacles fall by the wayside,
And never hang on to the fear.
Forgiveness is part of love.
It drives the anger away.
But take it one step at a time, my friends.
You know Rome wasn't built in a day.
Slowly but surely, let your heart mend,
And it does have to start with you.
The changes must come from the inside
Before you meet the real you.
Change your life here on earth.
Then progression will make you smile.
For a long journey starts with one small step
Before covering many a mile.

It's an everlasting life
With many a lesson to be learned along the way
And many new friends to meet,
So why not start your journey today?

Down on the Farm

There was hell on the Jenkins' farm last Christmas. The turkeys went on strike,
And one brave bird attempted to escape after stealing the farmer's bike.
He didn't get very far; he crashed into a five-bar gate
And ended up in gravy early this year, stuffed on the farmhouse plate.

So the turkeys held an emergency meeting, and the leader of the turkeys said,
"They filled our brother with sage and onion. I just hope poor Cecil was dead."
All the turkeys became very angry, and they formed a militant group.
Their slogan was "No turkey for Christmas. Why not have chicken soup?"

Now the chickens got to hearing about this, and the feathers started to fly.
Then the pigs were caught in the crossfire. They weren't even safe in their sty.
The ducks sided with the chickens, and when the fighting became intense,
The geese joined in on the turkeys' side, but the cockerel stayed on the fence.

The sheepdog hid in his kennel while the farmer ran for his life
After the sheep turned very nasty and the goat had butted his wife.
The fighting lasted for several weeks, and it spread to other farms.
Then the cows joined in the action, and even the bull took up arms.

The fighting spread throughout the country. Every farm in Britain was involved.
Then it suddenly ended just before Christmas, when everything was resolved.

The government agreed to all animal demands, so peace finally prevailed.
But the chickens still won't talk to the turkeys, and all mediation has failed.

So there'll be no turkey this Christmas. No chicken, goose, or duck.
There'll be nothing for you to stuff and nothing for you to pluck.
There'll definitely be no meat this year, so there won't be anything to roast.
So it's Welsh rabbit for Christmas dinner, but that's okay. I like cheese on toast.

Selfish Gain

This is the story of a selfish old man.
Being mean and spiteful was part of his plan.
He would boast and bluster every single day
About all the money he'd stashed away.
He would lie and cheat, provoke and steal,
And other people's pain he could never feel.
All his dreams were of his selfish gain.
He was never satisfied and would always complain.
Some said he was frugal; others said he was sound.
But they called him a miser when he wasn't around.
Then one day he realized that he was left on his own
Because of the bitterness that he had sown.
He was full of self-pity at being left on the shelf
And all because he only thought of himself.
And on the day he died there was no one to grieve.
No one noticed or cared that he'd taken his leave.
The vicar said a prayer as he was laid in the ground,
But this went unheard because no one was around.
In the end, all the wealth that this miser so prized
Was shared by the relatives he so despised.
So it's not about how rich or how famous you are.
There are much more important things by far.
It's about every heart you touch while on earth,
And it's all about showing your own true worth.
It's all about truth, and it's all about caring.

It's all about love, and it's all about sharing.
Our souls can progress every single day,
But it's up to each of us to live the right way.
There will be no reward for meanness or spite
Because only through love will we see God's light.

Self-Sacrifice

I wonder if God is male or female. Or does sex play no important part?
Is our creator an androgynous being, a great spirit with a greater heart?
The force that created this universe is a force of pure love,
And this spirit is all around us, not just in a place we call heaven above.

Pure love created this universe, and call it what you will,
But pure love has always been with us, and this love guides us still.
But many now seem to have lost their way; personal pleasure is the only creed.
The brotherhood of man doesn't exist for them, so they live and die for greed.

We no longer respect one another, even though we're from the same seed.
We must now learn to open our hearts by helping others in need.
Giving something of ourselves, with no thought of any reward,
Will always help us grow in the eyes of the one we call Lord.

Self-sacrifice builds your character. Giving of yourself is a wonderful gift.
When it's done with love, it's amazing and guaranteed to give all a lift.
Sacrifice involves unconditional love, and no love can ever be greater
Except for the love of all living things that comes from our creator.

This is how we should be living our lives. To this we must all aspire.
And through service to all of God's creatures, we progress ever higher and higher.
Caring in any way or form changes the person you are.
Character is built through sacrifice, and your eternal soul will shine like a star.

But here is a word of caution: your life is important, too.
Everyone must make his or her own mistakes, and obviously this includes you.
We must not live people's lives for them; for they would never learn or grow.
We should only help when it is truly needed, and that's all we need to know.

Do Not Judge

Do not judge less you be judged,
For how can you really tell
What another soul has been through?
It may be a life of hell.

Let them be who they are.
They have their own path to find.
They have their own mistakes to make.
To their problems you might be blind.

You must walk a mile in their shoes.
Well, that's how the saying goes.
And none of us are perfect;
We all make mistakes, heaven knows.

So live your life the best way you can.
Be an example to others, too.
Don't fall into idle gossip, my friends,
For that's the wrong thing to do.

We should live by our own moral standards,
And judging others is not the way,
For our time on earth is transient
And we don't have that long to stay.

Remember, to your own self be true,
And follow your path to the light.
Live your life without anger and hate
And your future is bound to be bright.

A Shoulder to Cry On

We can only understand the pain of others if we, too, have experienced that pain.
Unless you have had the same experience, don't offer advice; just refrain.
We should never give unsolicited advice about something we know little about.
So just listen to what they need to say; let them pour their feelings out.

Sometimes we are only meant to listen, so our advice won't be heeded.
Maybe they just want a shoulder to cry on and that will be all that's needed.
Quite often this is all that's required to help ease someone's pain,
The release of those hidden feelings that torment each of us now and again.

But sometimes we don't know who to trust if we don't have that special friend
To whom we all need to unburden ourselves, when a human soul needs to mend.
Hiding your feelings can cause great harm. Talking with a friend can be the cure.
But it must be someone who holds your trust, and you really do have to be sure.

If you have a special friend like that, you are very lucky indeed.
So treasure that friend of yours, and be aware of what they need.
Remember, friendship is a two-way street, so there needs to be give and take.
We should never abuse a friendship. That would be a grave mistake.

They say you can't choose your family, but you can choose your friends.
And it's always a very sad thing, indeed, when any friendship ends.

So treat your friends as if they are family. Be kind in word and deed.
Because the love of a friend is essential: it's a basic human need.

And if you have a partner, he or she should be your best friend bar none.
Then you will have that shoulder to cry on; in the darkest days they will
be your sun When you have a love like that, only death can tear it apart.
For when two become one, it lasts forever, soul to soul and heart to heart.

Reunited

When the time comes to make our final journey,
That inevitable trip back home,
A loved one will always come to fetch us
So we never have to travel alone.
Whether it's a parent
Or a loving partner who went on ahead,
All God's children should understand
That there's no such thing as dead.
Our lives on earth may be over,
But life's everlasting in God's kingdom above,
Where pain can no longer take root
And anger is banished by love.
Gone are the worries of an earthly life,
Gone is the bodily pain,
In a wonderful place of untold beauty,
Where we are all reunited again.
Friends and family will gather around
To welcome us back with a smile,
Saying, "Rest your head, weary traveler.
Come stay with us for a while."
And those who are left behind to grieve
I hope one day will understand
That a better life awaits us all
In our Father's Summerland.
There are two things that I'm sure of:
The fact that life can never end

And love can never ever die
Between you and yours, my friend.

Rich Man Poor Man

Once upon a time, there sat in an ivory tower
A very wealthy man who wielded so much power.
He had all the money he would ever need, for he was rich beyond compare,
And of other people's struggles, he was blissfully unaware.

All this wealth he had, he was very determined to keep.
And so what if the poor were suffering? He wouldn't lose any sleep.
If he could live to be a thousand, he would still have too much to spend,
But there was one thing he didn't possess—someone to call a true friend.

You see, he couldn't trust anyone, so he stayed single all his life.
He thought everyone wanted his money, so he never took a wife.
The only pleasure he ever had was the buying of some new toy,
But the novelty always wore off too soon, and nothing could bring him joy.

But everything he owned he made sure he kept. He didn't believe in giving.
This wealthy man might as well have been dead because he really wasn't
living.
We really ought to pity this man because, despite all his wealth and power,
He never knew the love of a good woman or saw the perfection in a flower.

He was blind to the beauty all around him. Simple pleasures passed him by.
And no matter how much money he had, he couldn't help but cry.
This man was incredibly lonely; there was no one he could trust.
His eyes were full of sadness because his heart had turned to dust.

Wealth isn't about the money we possess or even the treasures we own.
It's about our friends and family and never feeling alone.
It's about the things we do for others and about the love we give,
Because love is the be all and end all and the reason why we live.

Say a Prayer

Broken hearts, love, fear, and doubt—
That's what this earthly life is about.
Pain and pleasure in equal measure.
The missing loved ones that we treasure.
The pain of a mother that precedes the joy
Of a newborn baby girl or boy.
Sometimes we wish for our lives to end
Or at least that a broken heart would mend.
Other times we feel such incredible bliss,
A touch of a friend, or a loved one's kiss.
But life can be hard while on the earth we stay,
Until we return home one day
To a wonderful place where all life began
For all living creatures, woman and man.
There we'll meet our loved ones who went on ahead,
Who are so full of life that they can never be dead.
Only your body will remain on this earth
To be buried or cremated, for it no longer has worth.
The worms may feed on the empty shell,
But you will survive this earthly hell.
There is nothing of you that will have to stay.
Spirit and soul will be on their way.
That physical body was only for a lend.
You are spirit and cannot die, my friend.
And for all the loved ones you leave behind,
Please say a prayer for their lives to be kind.
And when you finally touch that heavenly ground,
Try to let them know that you're safe and sound
And that love survives beyond the grave
So that with this knowledge they can be brave.
There'll be no need for tears then, no need to cry.
The truth will free them: we cannot die.

Someone Up There Likes Me

I know someone up there likes me,
And I know this will sound a little profound,
But when you've promised to work for the light,
Angels and guides will gather 'round.

Every time I've thought, *I can't go on*,
I've heard spirit voices loud and clear,
And I know I'm being watched over
By those angels who often come so near.

As I've gradually become more aware
And understand the universal law,
I can see God's perfection in everything,
Even though some life experiences can feel so raw.

But hardship and pain are just building blocks
To help each single soul grow,
And coincidence plays no part in our lives.
This I've definitely come to know.

We are all inspired by spirit.
They help us whenever they can,
For they want us to succeed in our endeavors.
For spiritual growth is our Father's plan.

Everything I've gone through in this life
Has prepared me for what is to come,
For how could I possibly be of help to others
If of pain and hardship I'd had none?

How could I possibly understand grief
If in a carefree way my life had evolved.
And how could I possibly understand love
If in caring for someone I had never been involved.

Obviously this life has been hard at times,
But I'm told a silver lining is on the way.
So here I am patiently waiting, Lord,
Hoping and praying for that glorious day.

You know whatever doesn't kill you will make you stronger.
Believe me, that adage is true.
And friends, one day your body will die,
But always remember, your body's not you.

A Prayer for Peace

Father, give us the knowledge to emerge from the dark,
Proof that we are all connected by your divine spark.
Please give understanding to those in conflict with others.
Let them know they are fighting their sisters and brothers.
Bring faith to the faithless and open their eyes.
Bring truth to religion. Free it from lies.
Take love and compassion into every home.
Guide and protect us wherever we roam.
Give solace to the sad who suffer in silence.
Bring peace to those who have seen too much violence.
To all the earth's children, let them frolic and play.
Let their time to grow up be far, far away.
And for all the lonely, let new friends be found.
Let fellowship and joy freely abound.
And for all those with power, give them wisdom as well.
For without wisdom, they could create hell.
For all politicians, let their compassion be freed
So they can help those in the greatest of need.
Bring peace to all nations and an end to war.
Let them know there is nothing worth killing for.
To those in care and to those who are caring,
Please bring some relief from the hardship they are bearing.
Let cruelty to animals be a thing of the past,
And let love and peace surround them at last.

And for all those who grieve, let them now understand
That their lost loved ones abide in a wonderful land.
And for all those who live full of anger and strife,
Let them know that love is the only true meaning of life.
And for those who are in slavery, please set them free
And help them to forgive and to just let it be.
And finally, Lord, from all women and men,
Please forgive us our sins, dear Father. Amen.

The Ascension

I've been told that I've been very patient,
But now the time is here,
A time to forget about anger and sorrow,
A time to relinquish fear.
I've been told that a golden age is coming,
So I must believe that this is true,
A time of peace and love for me
And a time of peace and love for you.
This period in time has been foretold.
The ascension is now at hand.
This was always supposed to happen.
This has always been carefully planned.
More people believe in spirit now.
That's why the internet came into being.
Soon everyone will understand
Because of the evidence they are seeing.
Many have been waiting for this time
From the moment of their birth.
There are many now who will play a part
In the ascension of this earth.
We will have to leave the old ways behind.
Selfishness and greed must go.
Hate and racism will be cast aside,
And all negative feelings will be no more.

Many are going through these changes now,
Even some we cannot see.
Believe me, I know this is happening.
I can feel it happening to me.
I'm definitely not the person I was,
But then I was warned that I would change.
My senses are becoming far more acute,
And now everything seems so strange.

My emotions are closer to the surface now,
And there's a feeling of loneliness I can't shake.
I'm having these vivid dreams all the time,
And then suddenly I'm wide awake.
Even though I don't understand it all,
I've a feeling I've been waiting for this.
I know that something huge is coming,
And it's something I don't want to miss.
I must say I'm very excited,
More than I've ever been before.
I have witnessed so many incredible things,
And they keep on showing me more.
I cannot deny the things I have seen,
For that would be foolish, indeed.
So I know that changes are coming,
And for many people there is a great need.
We cannot go further in this direction,
For we were on the road to destruction.
Many are consumed with depravity and greed
And could pay for their seduction.
Many only care about themselves.
They no longer notice another person's pain.
The self has become so important now
That love is going down the drain.
The human ego has become a monster,
But not everyone has this affliction.
With God's help, those who do

Can cure themselves of this addiction.
So there is great hope for the future,
And many now will change their ways.
For them there will be a heaven on earth,
And then there will be no end of days.

The Pearl

The oyster is a lowly creature,
But there is a pearl that can grow inside.
You cannot see its shinning glory,
For in the darkness all light is denied.

But once the pearl is free from the shell,
Its radiance can be so bright.
Then it no longer needs the oyster
To hide its obvious beauty from sight.

We are the pearl inside the shell,
Never knowing fully who we truly are
Until the shell has been opened.
Only then will we travel far.

I'm not talking about the miles we travel
But about the progression we make
When we finally emerge from our shell
By following those first few steps we take.

A pearl is created through agitation,
And it's the same for the human soul.
We become stronger after all of life's trials,
And this eventually will make us whole.

We are meant to leave the shell behind
And to learn and progress with help from above.

Then our true nature will be revealed,
And we will only show each other love.

Our visits to the earth are all about growth,
Through hardship, pain, and grief.
And until we shuffle off this mortal coil,
We will never seem to find much relief.

But it isn't just about learning from pain
Or the situations we must go through.
It's about finding out who we really are
And trusting in love to guide us, too.

Death isn't what we think it is.
It's a new beginning in another place.
As an eternal being of pure light,
We are vastly improved after everything we face.

So why should we fear the body's demise?
Does the pearl miss its shell?
I won't miss my earthly encumbrance,
And I'll be glad to see the back of this hell.

I will only miss the people.
Nothing else will matter at all.
I will miss the contact with those I have loved
When I finally hear that heavenly call.

But I did ask for this life,
So I have only myself to blame.
We all need these lessons to move much higher,
And I chose them carefully before I came.

How you live each life is up to you.
You can stay on your path or stray.

And because of free will, we are all cocreators,
And God wouldn't have it any other way.

We can't blame God for the mess we are in.
We should take responsibility for everything we do.
And if we did this, the world would be a far better place,
And remember, my friends, he still watches you.

The Nature of the Beast

I was very confused when I was young, and my confidence was low.
Later there was so much sadness in my life that I feared another blow.

But everything that I am is yours, if you can find anything worth keeping.
Though there is a different man inside, who may still be sleeping.

Please be patient with me, my love. I've been hurting for quite a while.
I know I can start to live again, but first I need to learn to smile.

I hide the pain as much as I can, so everyone thinks I'm all right.
But when I'm on my own, I struggle, and I'm unable to sleep at night.

I know it's just this depression, and I shouldn't feel any shame.
I've been told I shouldn't blame myself, but I do all the same.

I didn't know depression felt like this. It comes as a wave crashing over me.
And even though I know it's coming, I can't get away, and I can't be free.

Once the wave hits, it drags me under. I feel like I'm drowning in tears
And the undertow won't release me. Then I'm surrounded by all my fears.

I feared it might happen when I wasn't alone, but that's not the nature of
the beast.
It seems to feed on loneliness. Well, it does with me, at least.

But now that I've met you, it's eased. You've frightened the beast away.
For the first time in years I don't need to pretend. I seem to be smiling all day.

Isn't it amazing what love can achieve? For love can stand any test.
It's the most powerful force in the universe, and once again I'm feeling blessed.

CHAPTER 11

Messages

A Message from Spirit via John

The following passage is a message received by my first spiritual teacher, John. He received this message while in an altered state, and he was told that the message was for me.

The following words are from spirit, and Gareth, what you must do is understand what the words in italics mean. This will help you to see what you cannot see with the physical eye.

These words will have a bearing toward all the knowledge that is waiting for you. But remember, there are two sides to every story—physical and spiritual. Understand the relationship between the two and then blend them together as you understand. Investigate the physical, meditate on the spiritual, and listen to what is said during meditation. Trust the thoughts that are given to you and accept them. It is irrelevant at this moment whether they are right or wrong. You must get into the habit of accepting that the words you receive come from spirit, and the more you accept, the more you will believe. This is what spirit is waiting for. They will guide you toward your true vocation. This is only the beginning, Gareth. You will amaze yourself with what you believe you can and will eventually do. Instruments are now being built to register the *vibrations of thought*, or *soul vibrations*, instruments that will be the means of demonstrating to humanity the reality of *invisible forces*.

Most people have in their homes a receiving set able to register the *waves* passing through the *ether*. When you press a switch, you hear music or see pictures coming, maybe from the other side of the earth, and you accept this as an ordinary happening. You speak into a telephone and your friend answers you from perhaps many hundreds of miles away, though you hear the voice as clearly as if they were in the very room in which you stand. These inventions are overcoming space and demonstrating that the *ether* is full of *waves of sound* and *waves of light*.

But there are other waves to which you are learning to respond. You are learning to be consciously receptive to *thought waves.* You are discovering that *you yourself are receiving stations* and that *through exercise of your mind and will, you can tune in to whatever station you desire*. You can *attune* yourself to rays from the angelic kingdom of beauty and light or to spheres of darkness, selfishness, and greed. Nevertheless, we must recognize that the forces of good and evil both proceed from the life of God. *Thought* is the most powerful agent; *all form originates from the mind*, from thought. We are trying to show you and help you because we love you; we are your companions in spirit. We have ways to travel beyond and beyond and beyond the earth, but so can you, Gareth. *You just need to open your eyes and see.* Sorry the writing is a bit shaky, but this was written in an altered state. All this information came through for you, Gareth. You will see that it is definitely your path for the moment, until the next stage.

Another Message from My Grandfather

Gareth, my boy, do not start doubting yourself again. You need to believe in the things that are happening. Remember, there are no such things as coincidences. You are beginning to understand how this is all working now, so don't fall back into your old doubting ways. We are never far away from you, and we constantly give you little hints. We know you are always going to pick up on these hints because you are now becoming more aware of who you really are. We are not human beings, Gareth, and we never have been, and we were never meant to live one single life. This is not who or what we are. We are all part of a vast network; we are each a part of a being that will one day lead us to become fully aware of our own divinity, and you are just a small but nevertheless important part of the whole.

Gareth, it has taken many lifetimes and such a long period in time to get to where we are today, and believe it or not, we are just getting started. Life goes on forever. It does, Gareth. I promise you this. And the things you see, touch, and sense are not all real. The only thing that truly exists is spirit; all the rest is just a mirage. The pain, the joy, the agony, and the ecstasy are real because these are feelings we all must endure, and in some cases, enjoy.

We need to sample every feeling and emotion there is, and we must become aware of each other's pain and feel sympathy, love, and wonder at every one of our sisters and brothers. Gareth, we will never leave you, my boy, because of the bond of love we have between us. We have been watching your progress ever since we crossed over to the greater side of existence.

At this time, you are living in a very dark world, and we wish nothing but happiness for you, but we know that if you only sampled the good things that a physical life can bring, then you would eventually become an emotionless cripple because the pain that life inflicts gives you the character you need.

All that pain and emotion you have experienced throughout your many lives has made you the person you are. Gareth, we are very proud of you. You have a strong character, my boy, and you always try to do the right thing and never let anyone down if you can help it. These characteristics are born in the flames of hardship that you have had to endure over many lifetimes. So don't worry, my boy, you are far stronger than you think you are, and we know you will prevail. It's just doubt coming back to haunt you again, though we don't doubt you. It's only the human part of you that gives you these feelings.

The human brain is a powerful tool that we are given on our earthly sojourn, but it can also have a detrimental effect on the spirit. But then, we are not meant to understand everything in this earthly form, or it would be a waste of time and energy coming here in the first place. If you could see what we can see, you would understand that this is only a trial of strength and knowledge. You are being tested, and you are doing well, my boy, so don't fall back into your old ways now that you are doing so well.

Gareth, there are still things you are meant to achieve, and we all believe in you because we have seen how you have dealt with everything that life has thrown at you. There is nothing you cannot deal with, my boy, because you are a very strong person.

A Message from Tina

Ask for knowledge of the future, and it will be yours, but you must ask for help from the angels, Gareth. This is very important for you now because the information you receive will explain everything for you. There is no need for you to be frightened at all, for you are going to be a teacher in the new world that will rise from the ashes of the old. You will teach others who we really are and why we populate this beautiful planet that is so special to the universe. There is no place in the entire universe like the earth. It is a very special place to which only those who need to make a great leap in their progression come.

You, on the other hand, have come mainly to teach, but you have also come to learn so that you will be able to teach and overcome this human experience by becoming your higher self while still locked inside your human body. This was meant to happen because, if it hadn't, then you could easily have slept through the entire human experience without ever waking from it and would never have become aware of the truth. Gareth, you will make great strides now that you are becoming far more aware. Do not be afraid to ask the angels, especially the archangels Michael for protection and Gabriel for knowledge. This is essential to you, my love, because the knowledge you need to do your work will all be there, ready for you, but as far as the angels are concerned, you must ask. We, on the other hand, will always be here, helping you to find the truth.

Gareth, you will now be made aware of many things that may even shock you, but you must not hesitate in believing what you will be told. So go forward now, my love, with confidence and bravery, for you are protected by all in the spirit world, who know exactly what you have promised to do.

Gareth W. Phillips

A Message from a Higher Being or Beings

I received the following message not long after I asked the archangels Michael and Gabriel for help.

I am a being of the light, and I come to this earth to work for the light, to lead others into the light, and to save those who would be saved by the knowledge of the light. I am a teacher, I am a healer, and I am a being from another world that wishes to help all of mankind. If mankind wishes me to help them, all they need to do is listen to my words, take in the things I say, and then use them for their own progression. I will help as much as I can, but it all depends on each individual being.

I am the light that cannot be seen with the human eye. I am the light that can only be seen through the soul. My light will shine for everyone, but it can only shine if that being is ready to see the light that I give. My mission is to teach and to help those who wish to be helped so that they can gain the knowledge of what is to come. I also seek to help them ascend to their rightful place, either in the world of spirit or here on earth so that they can help me teach others the true word that comes from the light.

I am part of the light and so is every living thing in this universe and in every other universe. We are all part of one vast entity that has lived forever. You are part of me, and I am part of you. I give my love freely to you so that you may give that love freely to others. May we all learn one day that love is the only answer that makes any sense. Go forward and live in love and light and know that I will have the same love for you that I have for all other beings of the light. My love is endless and contains everything that you will need to progress and become the very essence of the one who created you for the purpose of love and understanding of this one vast network of souls we call life. You are part of this vast network, a very important part, and one day you will astonish yourself with what you will be able to achieve in my name and in the name of all those you will be able to help.

My child, go forward with the knowledge that there is something far greater than every single one of us, something that connects us all together, something that will never deceive or hurt us but will instead care for us all as if we were part of its being, which in fact we are. My child, be aware

114

that you will be working with the light that comes and enters all of us at some time in our lives. You now have that light, and we wish you to use it wisely. We will be with you every step of the way, making sure no harm comes to the light worker who has found the calling that has awaited him for many lifetimes.

This is an important time for you, the most important time in your entire existence. You must be very aware by now that we have chosen you for a specific task. We will be making sure that you have everything you need to complete it.

You may now relax, my child, for I know this was a very strange experience for you. But we had to explain this to you at this time because, you see, we knew you were in just the right position and in just the right frame of mind to accept all of this. That is why it has happened now. We will be in touch again, Gareth, and that is a promise from one who loves you and has always loved you.

Another Message from a Higher Being

Being afraid isn't necessary, for life is to be enjoyed. Come with me and be who you truly are. Let me fill you with the love you need to enjoy even the sad moments, because so many do not need to be grieved for. You must celebrate the fact that they existed and brought love into your life and helped to teach you the lessons you needed. Celebrate their life, and love the feelings you still have for them even though you can no longer see them. Be as one with the everlasting certainty that they still exist, and know that they still love you, even with all your faults, because now they can see you as a perfect being in an imperfect body that is only here to learn about the true meaning of life.

And speaking of the true meaning of life, you are now able to understand because your brain doesn't govern your every waking thought, Gareth. Now your higher self is telling you how to behave and how to live, and is filling your whole being with love. You are becoming your higher self, and at first this will cause you great problems. You will feel things to a far greater degree. You will be hurt more easily because you are becoming more sensitive. You will want to express your feelings more now, and others may think you are becoming strange because all you will want to do is express love and feel love in return.

You are now beginning to understand the truth behind your journey of life. This life doesn't really exist as a reality. It is only a dream. And you are now awakening to the fact that you can work miracles if you believe you can. What others will see as strange, you will see as a possibility for change. What others will see as foolish, you will see as natural.

You are changing, Gareth, and every day these changes are becoming more evident. You will eventually become someone you never dreamed of becoming, and this will make you a special being because this was always meant for you. There is a time limit on this particular existence for you, Gareth, so everything you do now must flow with certainty, and only then will you hit all your targets.

You are here to help others in the name of the one who gave you life. Use his energy, which flows through you, and use the power and knowledge you are being given to enlighten those who seek you out. Don't waste time on those who do not wish to hear. Move on to those who are open and responsive to your words. Live the rest of this earthly life with the knowledge that you have our love and protection. Nothing can harm the real you, Gareth, so just have the confidence to be as we intended you to be. Spread his word, and let all your actions contain the love that is rapidly growing inside you. Be love, feel love, send love, create love, and live with love.

CHAPTER 12

Back to the Poems

The Loaded Weapon

Even someone who is unarmed can pose a threat.
The human body can become a deadly weapon.
But our most fearsome weapon is the spoken word.
Long after the scars from a fist have healed,
The wounds caused by spiteful words can linger on.
Sometimes these scars never completely heal.
Be careful how you wield this dangerous weapon
Because you will never understand its full power
And you may never see the harm it causes others.
Often the innocent are hurt as well.
Your tongue is a loaded weapon.
So please choose your words carefully.

If Only

If only we could be satisfied with what we already have.
If we could stop wanting more and more,
Eventually we would find true happiness
Because contentment is a most blissful state of mind.
If only we could learn to forgive those who hurt us.
If we could send love in our thoughts instead of hate,

We would surely find peace in our hearts
And learn the true worth of love.
If only.

The Hidden

We are here on this planet to learn,
And what happens isn't just fate,
For the earth isn't our natural home,
And this human body's not our natural state.
We are beings that come from the light,
And we're trapped in this physical form,
Here to learn through pain and hardship.
We are spirit beings that must learn in the storm.
Every bit of pain you go through
Will build your character, my friend.
You will become stronger with each new test,
And a higher being you will be at the end.
The real you cannot be harmed.
Only what you see in the mirror will age.
Only the mortal body will decay,
So death is freedom from the cage.
We should never be afraid of death.
It's a natural state of release.
When we shed this outer garment
And finally know a spiritual peace,
Only this body will go back to the earth,
And this is how it must be.
Each body we are loaned is for one short lifetime
And not for eternity.
So I'm not what you see on the outside.
None of us are. We are hidden within.
And when we reach our spiritual home,
Then our true life will again begin.
What you see here is not who I am.

I can't see you, and you cannot see me.
The real being of light stays hidden inside
Until that glorious day when we are set free.

The Mountains of My Home

I could never leave these mountains.
I will never tire of this magical place.
Its vibrant colors live in my heart,
And its beauty warms my face.

I've never been a happy wanderer.
I've never longed to roam.
For me, God lives in these mountains—
The only place I feel at home.

When I look up from the valley below
And see the ancient mountains that surround,
I know I'm in special place.
For me this is sacred ground.

I would never be able to breathe in a city.
Living that life would make me sad.
I would pine away in an urban dwelling,
Eventually becoming restless or mad.

I do occasionally feel drawn to the sea.
Maybe it's for something I lack.
But I always return to my valley home.
These mountains keep calling me back.

How I love this verdant country of mine,
With its valleys, mountains, and vales.
This will suffice until heaven calls.
This is my cymru, the land others call Wales.

The Olive Branch

The moments we regret from when we were young,
The things we said and the mud we slung,
We wish we could have curbed our tongue,
For we know better now.
The things we thought were important then
No longer mean what they did when
We were far younger women and men
And we were too blind to see.

But when someone special goes away,
Never to return another day,
Only then I know I'll hear you say,
"I regret what I said and did."
Perhaps one day you will agree,
For in hindsight we always see
The way that it was meant to be,
But by then it will be too late.

You'll wish you hadn't said those things,
For the harsher the words, the more it stings,
And you'll rue the pain your conscience brings
That could haunt you all your days.
So before you speak in angry haste
The words that leave a bitter taste,
This is a chance you should not waste
To offer the olive branch.

I know that you don't want to feel.
You think old wounds can never heal.
But it's your fate you're going to seal
If you can't or won't forgive.

You Get What You Give

I've been told that the love we receive
Is equal to the love that we give,
And this is true for everyone
For as long as we shall live.
If you have no love in your heart
And hate is what you render,
Your hatred will always come back to you.
It will always return to sender.
We always receive what we give,
And if the message you send is hate,
Your soul will always suffer,
So change before it's too late.
And if you actually hurt someone
Who doesn't deserve your spite,
Your conscience will make you ill
Until you decide to put this right.
You must always make amends
For every wrong you do.
You can't keep hurting people
Because of the anger inside you.
All you need do is say sorry,
Show remorse in your eyes,
Ask for their forgiveness,
Be sincere, tell no lies,
Love your fellow man,
Bring joy back into your life,
Open your heart and soul,
Then there'll be less trouble and strife.
So remember to give out love,
And you'll get it in return.
There is no need for hatred.
It's a lesson we all must learn.

Gareth W. Phillips

You Can't Hide from God

When I was older than I am today,
In a previous life in a land far away,
I had a different existence in every way
Which I sometimes have memories of.

Another life in another place,
With a different body and a different face,
On a distant planet somewhere in space,
So why do I see these things?

Am I seeing the future or is it the past?
I can't really tell; things are moving too fast.
They're over quite quickly; they don't seem to last.
But maybe one day I will know.

These other lives I sometimes recall
Are given as glimpses ever so small.
I'm just given a hint; I don't see it all.
Though hopefully one day I will.

We can live many lives, and we all volunteer,
But there is help from spirit, who always stay near.
So we really shouldn't have any great fear,
But so many don't understand

That our lives can never truly end
And that in our thoughts only love we should send.
But that's not so easy to do, my friend,
And that's one reason we keep coming back.

So through pain and hardship and even through stress,
We should always become more and never become less,
And every life that we live should help us progress,
For we are purified by the love we give.

This purification will take many lives.
Sometimes we'll be husbands and sometimes we'll be wives,
Though gender won't matter to the soul that survives,
For it's all about learning and love.

But some only feed on anger and hate.
To do others harm they would not hesitate.
They don't realize they will seal their own fate.
They are harming their immortal souls.

So the wicked who lie and are false behind backs
Are only just papering over the cracks.
One day they will pay for what their souls lack,
Because you can't defeat karma, my friends.

It's the universal law that is always applied:
You reap what you sow. It can't be denied.
And believe me, there is nowhere to hide.
Every bad deed will be seen.

You can fool other people. It's quite easy to do.
You can hide your true nature so no one sees you.
You can lie and cheat and never be true,
But you cannot hide from God.

Worry About the Living

We must worry about those who are left behind
And never feel sorry for the dead.
We must save our tears, my friends,
Save them for the living instead.
Worry about the lonely
And worry about the sad,
For the dead are not truly dead.
They're back home, so how is that bad?
Worry about the homeless

And worry about the poor.
Worry about the starving
Because they need our help for sure.
Worry about those in pain
Of the body or in the mind.
Worry about the helpless,
And then be sure to be kind.
Worry about our planet
Because not many seem to care,
And worry about the animal kingdom,
Who are mistreated, and that isn't fair.
Don't worry about the dead,
Because death is just a lie.
They are far more alive than we are;
The dead are not dead, and they cannot die.
They don't just live on in our memories.
They can see us every day,
And nothing can ever persuade them to leave.
They walk beside us every step of the way.
There are bonds of love that we share
That will last forever more.
They always stay very close to us.
They are just on the other side of the door.

The End of the Rainbow

Rainbow, you always lift my spirits
Whenever I'm feeling down.
You never fail to make me smile.
I'm so happy when you're around.

Everyone loves a rainbow.
It's a painting in the sky.
A masterpiece by God,
And its beauty can make you cry.

But the rainbow is also God's covenant
Between himself and man.
A reminder in the sky
Of our Father's eternal plan.

And as each human spirit evolves,
Its status in the rainbow is changed,
From violet to indigo and then to blue.
This has all been prearranged.

You then stay on this journey
Through green, yellow, orange, and red,
And with the help of our Father, God,
Our eternal spirit is fed.

And as you pass through each new stage,
The way you were is left behind,
And when you reach that rainbow's end,
You will feel a love for all mankind.

That's why we search for the rainbow's end
And why so many stories are told.
It's the ultimate reward for the human spirit.
It has nothing to do with a pot of gold.

The rainbow isn't just a phenomenon
Caused by some water and light.
It's proof of our covenant with God
And a wonderfully uplifting sight.

The pot of gold was just a hint
To help us achieve a glorious reward,
To find the true meaning of love,
And to finally gaze on the face of our Lord.

Bullying

You cannot make your own light brighter
By dimming someone else's flame,
For when you belittle another,
You will always bear the blame.
If you damage someone's self-belief
By harsh words said in spite,
You will hurt your own immortal soul
By believing you have that right.
Bullies are very sad individuals
Who often feel that they are inferior.
So by damaging someone with hurtful words or deeds,
They then feel this makes them superior.
This of course is false logic
Being used by a damaged mind,
By someone who is full of self-loathing
And has forgotten how to be kind.
They have probably been bullied themselves
At an earlier time in their life,
Leaving them feeling unworthy
And cutting them deep like a knife.
So the circle of spite continues,
And it has always been this way.
The bullied sometimes becomes a bully,
And another innocent becomes the prey.
But there is no need to become a bully.
The circle of spite can stop with you.
You don't have to perpetuate the misery
Because forgiveness works. It's true.
Just forgive those who bullied you.
See them as victims, too.
End the circle of malice and spite.
It's the right thing to do.

The Little Angel

Her family stood by the open grave as she was laid to rest.
Everyone had done what they could, and the doctors had done their best.

There were oh so many tears as her brothers and sisters cried
Because she was only eight years old when their little angel died.

But there were two souls at the service that no one there could see.
One was that little angel herself, and the other one was me.

I was her great grandfather, a relative she didn't know.
I led her into the light, where this beautiful child had to go.

And when the funeral was over, I took my great granddaughter's hand,
And led her back to her heavenly family because this is how it was planned.

This angel had learned all her lessons in many lives lived in the past.
She was a very old soul indeed, who will now stay in heaven at last.

And among her heavenly kinfolk, she'll watch over her family on earth,
Waiting in the light for her loved ones, watching every death and rebirth.

As I put my hand on her shoulder, she looked up and gave me a grin.
All her trials and tests were now over, and her heavenly life would begin.

Her life will be everlasting and her wisdom put to great use.
This little angel may become your guide, the one to teach you the truth.

For once we have learned all our earthly lessons, only then we can stay
To become a being of pure light and love in a heavenly place not far away.

The Inner Light

If you are searching for God,
Start by looking deep within yourself.

127

And when you have found that inner light,
You have discovered who you really are:
A spiritual being that is part of the great spirit that we call God.
But finding your spiritual self isn't the end.
Now you must let that inner light shine for all to see,
And then you will become a beacon for others.
Let your inner light shine for everyone without exception,
And the great spirit will always smile on you.

A Word to the Wise

A stupid man needs to tell everyone how clever he is.
He will boast and lie about his achievements.
A wise man remains silent and listens.
He never has to tell others who he is.
People will come to know his worth by his deeds,
So have the confidence to just listen.
Let your intellect sort the wheat from the chaff,
And then only speak if you have something important to say.
When a wise man or woman speaks, you can hear a pin drop.

The Inner Voice

Some say that life is full of pain.
Some say we die and are born again.
Some say we merely turn to dust.
Others will say in God we trust.

Some say we must all believe as they do.
Some say that's rubbish; others say it's true.
Some say we are all bound for hell.
Others say heaven. Who can tell?

But no matter what people say or do,
You must trust yourself to know what's true.

If it doesn't feel right, then walk away
And live to fight another day.

It's all right to listen to what others say,
But then follow your heart, for this is the way.
We all have an inner voice inside,
Our higher selves that can't be denied.

Try living with love, not anger and wrath.
Then trust your instincts and follow your path.
We've been given free will to make our own choices.
We've been given our minds and our voices.

Use them well. Don't waste any gift.
Don't cause someone pain. Don't cause a rift.
Because one day you will see and understand
That everything we go through has been planned

By a far greater being than you or I,
And because of his love, we can never die.

CHAPTER 13

Other Messages

A Message from Lewis

I was getting ready to go to our spiritual circle at Hayley's house when I suddenly started to get inspirational writing in the form of a poem. This often happens to me and can come from one of three different sources: my wife Tina, my grandfather Thomas, or someone I like to refer to as a higher being. Don't ask me how, but I knew it was from my wife Tina. She gave me about twelve lines of poetry, which I quickly wrote down on scraps of paper.

The poem was about Hayley's son Lewis, who had died at the tender age of five. So, as I was about to go to see Hayley, I took the poem with me and showed it to her. When I returned home, I started to work on the poem straight away, and over the next few days I altered my part of it several times until I was satisfied with it. I then printed it out and put it into a photo frame for Hayley.

I get a lot of inspiration from the other side. Sometimes poems are completely from spirit, at other times they are joint ventures, and sometimes I write the poems myself. But even the poems I write myself are still inspired by spirit because the idea is planted inside my head.

Now our circle meets every Tuesday afternoon, so on the following Tuesday morning, I was woken at around six o'clock by the usual sound of a spirit phone ringing. I assumed this was my grandfather, who usually wakes me in this way. But I was wrong. It was Lewis, and he gave me the following message:

> Gareth, thank you for the poem that you are going to give my mother. I have already thanked Tina for her part in this. Gareth, I know you hold my mother in high regard, and when you give her the poem, please tell her I have heard her prayers and will always love her.

When I came out of my altered state, I looked at the message to see what I had written and noticed that the writing was much larger than when my grandfather was the messenger. This had obviously been Lewis letting me know it was him. The following poem is for Lewis:

An Old Soul

A beautiful boy with a lesson to teach,
He came from a place not far out of reach.
He was an old soul with very little to learn,
Showing love and awareness he had to earn.

So very young but oh so wise,
You only had to look into his eyes.
Without any fear, he lived his short life,
Teaching lessons with love to a husband and wife.

His mother and father and brothers, too,
Taught these harsh lessons by one brave and true.
Yes, grief is a lesson. It's just part of living,
Like illness or stress, love or forgiving.

So don't be too sad or ashamed to cry,
For you know that his spirit is always close by.
Call out his name and say it with pride.
He will always love you, for he has not died.

We are all immortal. This is a fact.
And there's no such thing as the final act.
So his spirit lives on without any pain,
And on one glorious day you'll be with him again.

Tina and Marie

My wife Tina, who passed away in July 2007, often uses music to contact me with a message. Sometimes the message is obvious, but sometimes I must find the song's lyrics to understand what she wants me to know. The first time this happened to me was about fourteen months after her passing.

During those first fourteen months, I was in a terrible state and didn't really want the rest of my life. Then suddenly I heard a song from the late '50s or early '60s by Triny Lopez called "Gonna Get Along Without You Now." Now, this song got on my nerves, but I heard it several times a day, day after day, until this idiot finally realized what Tina was trying to tell me: *You got along without me before you met me, so you can get along without me now.* This was the first of many messages in song from Tina. The two songs discussed below are probably the most important ones so far.

Back in August 2011, I once again started hearing the same song over and over again, and every morning while making my breakfast, I would find myself singing this song. By now, of course, I had come to know that this was Tina's way of giving me a message because of my love and knowledge of popular music. The song I kept hearing for over a week was "The Day I Met Marie" by Cliff Richard, and when that song stopped, it was replaced by a Tony Christie song called "Amerilo," which contains the line "… and sweet Marie that waits for me." Now, it didn't take a genius to work out that I was going to meet someone called Marie.

A few days after the second song stopped, Marie walked into our church, and there was an instant connection between us. It was as if we had known each other all our lives, and that doesn't happen to me very often.

I didn't find out her name until a few weeks later, and I thought to myself, *This can't be the Marie I've been told of,* because she was twenty years younger than me, but six months later I asked Marie to go out with me despite the age difference. And the unlikely happened: she said yes. Unfortunately for me, she later changed her mind, so I thought maybe spirit was just telling me that we were going to be friends and nothing more. So I told Marie to forget I had asked her out and suggested we just be friends. A few weeks later, I attended a psychic supper, and a lovely medium from Hereford called Sue Moss told me that a woman called Marie would become very important in my life. A few days later, I tried to tell Marie this, but she didn't really want to listen to what I had to say, so I just gave up.

About four months later, I started to go out with my friend Madeline, who was about to move nearly two hundred miles away to Horsham in West Sussex. Because we had to travel so far to see each other, most of the time I was still on my own. During this time, Marie and I visited different churches as friends. My relationship with Madeline was good at first, but later I became unsettled because I knew through spirit that I was supposed to be with Marie.

Then something strange happened in the Glynneath Spiritualist Church. A medium I had not seen before linked Marie and me and predicted that we would one day be together as partners. This was just the first of many messages linking the pair of us. I had never told Marie about the feelings I still had for her because I didn't know if she felt the same in return. Then one day, a friend of mine who often gets messages from spirit told me that my wife Tina wasn't happy with my present relationship. This then led to another friend telling Marie and me that we were supposed to be together.

At this point, Marie and I had been members of the same circle for quite some time, and on a couple of occasions I had given Marie a message saying that I was being told by spirit that she was in love with someone, and Marie would then answer me by saying, "Yes, but he's in a relationship with someone else, and I would never try to break up someone's relationship." When I found myself giving her that message, it came out of my mouth before I realized what I was saying. (Sometimes it just happens like that.) As I realized what I had said about her being in love with someone, my stomach churned, my heart sank, and I felt terrible. Little did I know at the time, Marie was talking about me. It turns out Marie regretted saying no to me within a few months of me asking her out, and she thought she had blown any chance of us being together.

Well, in the end it was spirit that brought us together, and I can't remember being this happy for a very long time. We both waited for this to happen, and having to wait has made it all the sweeter.

A Poem for Pauline

I was sitting in my flat on my own reading a book about healing one day when the phone rang. It turned out to be my friend and fellow circle member Pauline, and she sounded very excited. She told me that her father, Derrick, had contacted her from spirit and had said that Gareth would write a poem for her and that she should phone me and ask me to do it.

Well, when she asked, I had no idea what to write about. I mean, I had never written a poem to order before, but I said I would give it a try. I didn't know if it was going to work because you cannot demand anything from spirit. You can only ask. So I asked. After asking for help, I picked up a pen and my writing pad, and to my great surprise, I felt as though I had entered an altered state almost straight away. I felt very, very strange, indeed. After I had finished writing the poem, I sat there feeling light-headed for quite a while before I looked at what I had written. I was quite shocked when I saw what was on the paper.

Pauline had been given a message in the church a few years earlier about a child she had lost, so I knew she had a child on the other side. But then again, I didn't write this poem; I only held the pen. Another thing about this poem is that I did have a connection to Pauline's family and knew her father very well, having lived next door to him and worked with him for many years. So Derrick would not have had a problem telling Pauline to ask me to do this for her, because he knew I would do it without even thinking about it.

The poem that follows was written through me, by spirit.

Twinkle, Twinkle, Little Star

Twinkle, twinkle, little star.
I have often wondered how you are,
A lost child that I never met,

A sad feeling of regret.
One day I know I'll see your face,
For in my dreams we both embrace,
And when I sleep upon my bed
My body lies as if it were dead.
That's when I journey to the other side,
For a mother's love won't be denied.
Reunited while my body is at rest,
I'll hold you close unto my breast.
Flesh of my flesh, being of light,
I can always find you in the night,
But I can't remember when I return
Back to my body, for there's more to learn.
But when all my lessons are over and done,
I'll take my place with you in the sun.
Flesh of my flesh, being of light,
I'll be dreaming of you again tonight.

I fervently hope that this poem written through me by those in spirit, who love and watch over all of us, helps at least one grieving mother, and hopefully more than one, to realize that life goes on in a place where her child is loved and cared for, and that she will certainly see her son or daughter again.

CHAPTER 14

A Few More Poems

The Caviar Isn't Up to Much

Greedy men with pitiless eyes
Sit at tables that overflow
While ignoring the starving all around them,
And nothing of that hunger will they ever know.

With their bellies near full to bursting
And no room for a conscience inside,
Their souls contain nothing but sand—
A desert for their pride.

Greed is the God they serve,
And they worship every penny.
While starvation grips much of this world,
Their crumbs would feed so many.

It would be nice the next time you eat at your trough
And pause to wipe the gravy from your chin,
If you thought of the children who won't see tomorrow
And then ask God to forgive you your sin.

Questions

I wonder how many lives I have lived
And how many earthly bodies I've known.
How many times have I loved you
Only to be left on my own?
How many times has my spirit found you
Only to lose you again?
Did I ever live a life without you?
Did I ever suffer that pain?

How long do I have to wait
Until I return to your side?
And how many times have I grieved for you
After your earthly body had died?
And how many times have you been hurt?
How many times have you cried for me,
Blinded by your tears,
Weeping so much you could hardly see?

Are our spirits gradually learning?
And how many tests have we passed?
How many lifetimes did we fail,
And how long will this one last?
So many unanswered questions,
So many puzzles to solve,
Before we begin to understand
That we go through these lives to evolve.

But I believe I know where our future lies.
We eventually stay in the light.
Life then becomes joy everlasting,
And never again will we fear the night.

Suffer to Serve

When we go through this earthly life
And are tossed around in the storm,
We don't realize that love is all we need
To keep us safe and warm.
This knowledge comes from quiet moments
With those who have gone before,
And they will gladly try to help us
From the other side of the door.
But if you are meant to work for spirit,
Then you must learn through hardship and pain.
For without the knowledge and understanding,
All your words would be in vain.
How can we help other people
If we haven't been through the same things, too?
For our words would fall on deaf ears every time
Because of a lack of understanding in me and you.
If you've never been through the mill,
How could you possibly begin to understand
What someone else is going through
Because you have no experience firsthand?
So never give someone free advice,
If you don't have that knowledge at all,
Just to make yourself look important.
All you're really doing is being very small.
That's why this life can be so hard
For those who are part of God's plan,
For without all the pain and torment,
How can you help your fellow man?
And you must be careful how you use your gift
Because if you let your ego win the day,
you may lose that gift from God.
It can be very easily taken away

Safe with Spirit

There is no death
Because life cannot end,
And the loved one you're missing
Watches over you, friend.
I feel for your loss
As I feel for my own.
We are all God's children,
Whether young or full-grown.

They are quite safe in spirit,
With their family above.
You may well feel their presence.
They still carry your love.
Please believe these words
Because I know they are true.
My wife is still with me,
As your loved one is with you.

Your grief's a heavy burden,
Though it will become lighter.
But you need to be strong.
You must now be a fighter.
We will see them again.
This isn't good-bye.
Life is everlasting,
So try not to cry.

One day they will come for us.
I believe this to be true.
My loved one for me
And your loved one for you.

The Ego Slave

We can all feel like islands,
Each one set adrift.
We think we are a single entity,
Never knowing that this is God's gift.
For we must live this life
To move forward and progress,
And no matter what we experience,
We will always become more, not less.
We enter this world as I,
And this is how we behave.
A single-brain controlled being,
To the ego we are ever a slave.
It must be this way while on earth,
For we learn in this human shell.
So we think that we are all islands,
And this can often feel like hell.
But it's just till the end of this lifetime
That we will all feel like this,
For in heaven we are all connected
In a world of heavenly bliss.
In spirit, we are all as one.
We are never alone, you see.
We are so much more than islands,
And one day we will all be free.
But while on this earth remember,
The real you will always survive,
For we are powerful spiritual beings
That one day will feel much more alive.
This earthly life is just a dream
Compared to what lies ahead,
So don't let fear ruin the experience,
Because there's no such thing as dead.

Understanding

I understand life more now, Father.
Life is hard, and that's a fact.
And we spend most of our life fearing death,
Never knowing there is no final act.

This world we live in can be terrifying,
But I now understand that you're not to blame,
Because you gave us free will at the outset,
So how we behave creates our own shame.

We are beings that have come from the light,
Our memories of heaven wiped clean.
We no longer know who we are
Or any of the lifetimes we've seen.

I know this is how it must be,
For if we were privy to what lie ahead,
Avoiding life's pitfalls would be simple,
But then all our progression would be dead.

But I wish to understand why I'm here
Because I want to be all I can be.
But as you know, Father, I lack some patience,
And this has always been a problem for me.

I am trying very hard to be patient,
But frustration is my constant foe,
For I know I am here for a reason,
And I know that I've been here before.

I know that we are all in the same boat
And progression for all is the aim.
We are here to learn through personal hardship
As we are playing this earthly game

For this is what it really is—
A game of hide-and-seek,
A chance to build our character
And no longer feel so weak.

And it's a spiritual weakness that we have at the start
That can only get stronger with each hardship we face,
Giving us a chance to be godlike,
To have unconditional love and grace.

Our real existence will be hidden from most
Until returning home once more,
And we will never truly understand the whole story
Until we close that earthly door.

But our earthly lives are essential
And so is the hardship and pain
Until love envelopes us completely,
And this, my friends, is the name of the game.

For it's not about who you are now;
It's about being all you can be.
It's about learning through every lifetime
By setting your higher self free.

The Wrong Direction

The more we earn, the more we spend.
This has become the human trend.
The things we want, those possessions we crave,
Are turning us into the consumer slave.
We want and we want until we finally get.
Then we wish we hadn't bothered and live to regret.
It will rarely get used, so we put it away,
Saying it will come in handy if we need it someday.
Consume, consume, we've all gone mad

For the latest gadgets, and isn't that sad?
We throw things away that are still working well
To buy the next model in consumer hell.
Put it in a landfill and then cover it with earth,
Or even fly tip it, if you can't see its worth.
It wasn't always like this in our past.
We had to be frugal, so things had to last.
Where will this end, this time fired by greed?
Remember the days when we were driven by a need?
We can't keep on going in this crazy direction.
Behind mountains of waste we've lost our connection.
Commercial television, we're seduced by its lies,
But a time must come soon when we open our eyes.
We are destroying our planet by soiling our nest.
The species known as humans are becoming a pest.
We dump toxic waste in sea and lake,
Knowing there's only so much that Mother Earth can take.
We are destroying our planet because we take without giving,
And we still expect it to go on living.
The earth is alive, not a rock floating in space.
I can't believe what's happening to this human race.
We're greedy, we're violent, and we've lost our way.
So let's hope we see sense before we're all blown away.

The Child You Never Knew

This is from the child you never really knew,
An all too brief gift in pink or blue,
A message from heaven for all fathers and mothers,
And we must not forget our sisters and brothers.
Whether we were miscarried, aborted, or even stillborn,
Our loved ones on earth will still have to mourn.
But we were never meant to touch this earth.
This was always about teaching, not about birth.
We came to teach lessons that will help you progress.
Our lives were short, but nevertheless,

We taught with love, but the lesson brought pain.
Though when the time comes, we will meet again.
We came for a purpose; we came to teach.
Now we grow up in heaven, not far out of reach.
We are cared for and nurtured and we watch from above
We are now with your families, who surround us with love.
Only you will suffer with the pain of grief
That comes in the night and steals like a thief
But it's all for a purpose, and we want you to know
That the meaning of life is to love and to grow.
Through earthly hardship, you will grow every day,
And you will learn through loss, for this is the way.
But do not be sad, for the pain will ease,
For we are always with you. Remember this, please.
It was a very harsh lesson, but it had to be taught,
And knowledge like this can never be bought.
When in spirit, you will see; you will come to know
That the harsher the lesson, the more we grow.
And for all our mothers who carried us inside,
We wish you to know that we have not died.
Be at peace. Dry your tears. We are not far away.
We are your children in spirit, and we will meet one day.

The Doorway

The human body is just a vehicle that's driven by our spirit and soul.
Each vehicle is driven until it fails, because evolution is spirit's goal.
And each time we return in human form, there's new transport to help us move,
Often no better than the last one we had, for only the soul will improve.

The heart is just an engine; our legs are nothing but wheels;
And the brain is the on-board computer. So we know how this vehicle feels.
The food we eat is just fuel, and drink's the lubrication we need.
Without these, the vehicle cannot work, and that's why we must feed.

We need this human vehicle to learn while on this earthly plane,
And we need this physical experience. That's why we return time and again.
But we need to look after this shell of ours, or our lives will end in dismay,
And then the grim reaper will have to come early to help us on our way.

That's when our loved ones will suffer, after seeing us lose our battle with life.
After Father Time says, "That's your lot," they can go through all sorts of strife.
And when we lose a loved one ourselves, we sometimes lose control.
Grief spreads through every fiber of our being because we don't understand the soul.

For only the body has turned to dust. Your loved one's spirit is still intact.
Life is truly everlasting, my friends, and this is not fiction but fact.
The soul will continue its journey; only its transport has died.
And death is just a doorway back to our maker's side.

You haven't lost your loved ones. They are watching while you grieve,
Hoping that you'll one day find out that they will never ever leave.
You will always see them again, for the human soul cannot die,
And because our lives are everlasting, there should be no reason to cry.

But we do cry because we miss them, and that's not hard to understand.
But remember, they still watch over us from God's glorious Summerland.

A Better Place

We live our lives
And then go on our way
To a far better place,
The wise one's say.
Free from harm,
All pain dissolved,
Free from care,

All problems solved.
Bathed in love,
With peace of mind.
It's the greatest experience
We'll ever find.
In a different dimension,
But still very near,
That has no sadness
Or any great fear.
So live your life
Without any regret.
Live with love
And never forget,
There is no hell,
No matter what you're told.
Only heaven awaits you
With its gates of gold.

Love Is Forever

We are all on a journey
Filled with joy and tears,
But then at life's end
A new world appears.

We see a bright light
And then we're on our way.
We are homeward bound
Many would say.

Gone is the pain
Along with all dread.
Heaven has claimed us,
So we're not really dead.

We're in the father's kingdom,
Surrounded by love
With all those we have missed
Up in heaven above.

But for those left behind
Who will all shed a tear,
I'll tell you this, my friends,
Your loved ones are still near.

Because love is the answer,
And love cannot die.
It links us forever,
And that isn't a lie.

Love is everlasting.
It can never fade.
For in the image of our creator,
One and all we were made.

A Place in the Sun

I cannot take my place in the sun
Until my time on this earth is done.
I cannot become the being inside
Until in heavenly realms I once more abide.

More lessons to learn that will polish my soul.
Higher and higher then back to the fold.
All that I vowed has not yet come about,
But with time, it will. I have no doubt.

Father who created this universe,
This time without you has seemed like a curse.
There were often times I pleaded and cried,
"Please take me back to be at your side."

Then I heard a voice saying, "Your time will come
When once more you will live your life in the sun.
Have patience, my child, and be at peace.
You have much more to learn before blessed release

To be with your loved ones who went on ahead
And to watch over others who may believe you are dead.
But they, too, will know when their time has come
That everyone will have his or her place in the sun.

The Unknown Soldier

I am the unknown soldier
Whose bones rest in an unmarked grave.
I can still remember how I died.
I was scared, but I tried to be brave.

It doesn't matter which side I fought on
And it doesn't even matter which war.
I wasn't sure why I was fighting
Or the reason for the carnage I saw.

I didn't even hate my enemy,
This man from a foreign land,
But I was fighting for my life
And for a cause I still don't understand.

I was never an angry man,
But I was given a weapon and taught to kill.
Now I pray for forgiveness for the blood I spilled
And release from the memories that haunt me still.

The powerful men who start these wars
Will never have to fight.
They sit and watch the results of their folly,
Never doubting that they were right.

But my soul is old and has lived many lives,
So I know that war is a waste.
I can see everything more clearly now
Because I'm in a better place.

War is brutal and futile,
And no lasting peace is ever achieved.
There is nothing glamorous about a war.
Just ask all the families who have grieved.

So now I watch from the kingdom of heaven
And I pray that man will discover
That we are all here to learn about love
And not to kill each another.

We have a spark deep inside us,
That each of us is meant to find
A piece of the divine spirit, I'm told,
That is destined to save humankind.

But until that time comes,
Mankind will still be fighting these wars.
Brother will still slaughter brother
And all for a worthless cause.

If only the people who have all the power
Could be given wisdom as well.
Then this world of ours would feel like heaven
Instead of feeling like hell.

The Everlasting

I know exactly where I'm going, so I'm not afraid to die.
You won't see a tear from me, because it won't be a time to cry.
And when that time arrives, I'll be coming back home to you,
Returning at the end of the day, just like I used to do.

I pity those poor people whose lives must be so bleak,
Especially when they get older and are feeling infirm or weak.
They fear the end of their lives; they dread that final demise.
They think they know what's coming, but they're in for a big surprise.

They think that dust awaits them. If they could only comprehend
That the spirit goes on forever, and that life doesn't actually end.
We pass from solid to spirit; it's a process that happens time and again.
And when the time comes to return home, there is little if any pain.

But they can't stop seeing death as the end; they think it's the final defeat.
But nothing begins or ends because a human heart fails to beat.
And when we lose a loved one and we're left with a broken heart,
It can be the end of the life that we knew, but it can also be a fresh start.

When your old life ends, then another life must begin,
And if you don't make the best of it, then, brother, that's a sin.
If you could look at it that way, then the pain wouldn't be so bad.
So try to remember the good times and all the love you've had.

You will meet your loved ones again, as sure as night follows day,
For we are all part of an everlasting cycle, and God has designed it that way.
But you do have to feel for those poor souls, living their lives through a lie,
Constantly missing out on living because they're so scared to die.

But, you see, energy can't be destroyed, and that's what we truly are.
We are citizens of the universe who have journeyed so very far.
I think of God as the ultimate recycler, so I don't have any fear,
And if you believe in the everlasting, then all thoughts of death will
disappear.

CHAPTER 15

Strange Days

After a period of time when I hadn't been getting as much as I was used to getting from spirit, probably because I was very busy with family problems, all of a sudden things changed quite dramatically with Marie and me. Strange things started to happen, first to Marie and then to me.

The first episode happened at home. Marie sometimes goes to bed before me, and on this particular night she woke up thinking I had gotten into bed without her knowing because she felt a presence next to her. She turned toward me, or what she thought was me, only to find an elderly Native American man lying next to her in bed; his arms were down by his sides, and he looked as if he were sleeping. Marie told me that she then heard a noise behind her and turned to see what was making the noise, but there was nothing there, and when she turned back to look at the old Indian, he had disappeared. Later, she gave me his description, and it turned out to be one of my guides, who I had seen on one occasion myself.

The second episode again concerned Marie and another guide of mine, a little Indian boy from the subcontinent. Marie was in the kitchen, and as she turned around, she saw him running through our passageway. I have never seen him myself, but I have been told about him by a well-respected medium called Marlene Abercrombie, who is a friend of ours. It isn't unusual for Marie to see spirit beings. She often sees them, and it has become quite normal for her. So it doesn't bother Marie at all. She can sometimes see a medium's guide standing next to him or her while the medium is working in a church, and she can often see people's auras as well.

The third incident was the strangest of all. This one happened on our trip to Disney Land Paris in May 2015. Believe it or not, we left a very sunny South Wales and arrived in Paris during the monsoon season. It rained every minute of our holiday except for one afternoon. Luckily, I had taken a rainproof jacket with me, but everyone else seemed to be buying ponchos. On our second night there, Marie had a very strange experience. She usually snuggles up to the back of me until she gets too warm and then turns to face away from me. Well, on this night, she turned her back to me only to find that I was on the other side of the bed as well. She turned back and forth several times and found herself trapped between two of me—a very frightening experience for her, considering Marie is claustrophobic. Marie shouted, "Stop this!" and turned around again to see me standing by the window, staring at her. Obviously there could not have been two of me. I mean, one is bad enough.

So the only explanation I can come up with is that my spirit had left my body and Marie had witnessed it. Needless to say, Marie had a problem going back to sleep after that, and my snoring didn't help much either. Marie's spirit very often leaves her body to visit her mother on the other side, and I have woken in the middle of the night next to her thinking was she okay. Her body does seem quite lifeless during these times. She makes no sound at all. The very first time I noticed this, it worried me, but I have become used to it. Marie visits her mother in the same place every single time: They meet in the most spectacular garden I have ever seen. The flowers are huge and more colorful than anything we can see on this earth. There are colors there that don't even exist on our planet. It is incredible to behold.

I know this not because Marie told me but because I was taken there by spirit to allow me to see Marie's special spirit place, because spirit knew that we were becoming one. We are all able to do this, but most people don't remember or they dismiss it as a vivid dream. I have also had these experiences myself but not as often as Marie. I think Marie is a frequent flier without ever needing an airplane.

Incident number four occurred three days later, back in sunny Aberdare. (Yes, it was still sunny in my hometown). This time it was my turn to have a bit of a shock. I woke from a deep sleep thinking that Marie had gotten out of bed. I sat up and watched her walking toward the bedroom door.

"Where are you off to, love?" I asked, and from the bed, lying next to me, Marie said, "What did you say?" So now there were two Maries as well.

We sat up in bed for a while talking about what had just happened, and we both agreed that I deserved that shock for what had taken place in Paris. Then we both went back to sleep. Later that same night, I was awoken again, this time by someone trying to pull me out of bed by my arm. A few days later, I had the very same experience again, minus the arm-pulling incident.

Incident number five occurred about two months later. Marie was dreaming, and in this dream, she noticed that I had a very long, thick black hair on my left leg. In her dream, she curled the hair around her finger several times and then yanked it out. Believe it or not, my left leg shot out in real life and kicked Marie. This didn't even wake me up from my deep sleep, and I slept on, oblivious to what had just happened.

The sixth incident happened to Marie while I was fast asleep in the next room. We had just moved into our new home after my aunt Margaret passed away just before Christmas 2016 and left me her house. This was the house I was born in and where I had spent the first seven years of my life. I have many happy memories of living in this house with my grandparents and parents, so I had no trouble settling in. However, Marie found it hard at first. She also found my uncle Alan's old bed a bit hard as well, so now and again she slept in the other bedroom on the smaller bed. On this particular night, she was awoken by two children playing in the bedroom. They were playing very loudly with a hoop and stick and continuously running up and down the stairs.

So Marie told them not to wake me and to play downstairs, which they did. After Marie described these two children to me later, I knew who they were straight away. The little boy of about six years old was my grandmother's brother little Davy, and the girl who was a year older was my grandfather's little sister, who has contacted me through several mediums before. Unfortunately, no one remembers her name. I hope that one day she will contact me again and tell me.

The seventh incident happened while I was giving a message to someone in the Aberdare church. When I'm giving a message, I like to move around. While moving around, I tripped over something on the left side of me. Without thinking, I looked down and for some reason I said,

"Sorry." I then looked at the congregation and said, "Why did I say sorry? There's nothing there." That was when my guide told me that I had tripped over a spaniel. So I asked the lady who was receiving the message if she had a family member who had owned a spaniel, because I'd just tripped over him. She laughed and said, "Yes, it was my father's dog." That had never happened to me before, but at least it made everyone in the church laugh and raised the vibration for the rest of the service.

The eighth incident occurred only a few days later in a different church. I was giving healing to a friend who was going through quite a few problems and at that time was having terrible trouble with hot flushes. After the healing, I asked spirit in my mind to please send a cold breeze for this lady, and to my astonishment, the breeze came before I had even got to the word *breeze*. Spirit always seems to be one or two steps ahead of us, so I don't know why I was so surprised, really.

That absolutely freezing cold breeze came from a bare wall that had no windows or doors. My friend and I looked at each other in total amazement, and I could see that she was obviously thinking the same as me: *Where did that come from?* At the time of this writing, there have been no more incidents. But I don't think it will be the last time spirit plays tricks on us.

CHAPTER 16

And More Poems

The Master

The master is more than one single soul.
To be as the master, this is our goal.
He is far more than one single being,
And we're all part of the one who is all-seeing.

You can see him in the smile of a very young child
And in all creatures, tame or wild.
You can see him in a brilliant new sunrise,
Or you may find him in your partner's eyes.

See him clearly in the dew on a rose,
Or you could find him in ten tiny toes.
You can find the master in the stars at night
Or in the sun and moon that shine so bright.

You can find him in your true love's embrace.
A baby will find him in its mother's face.
You can also find him in the birds that sing.
You can see the master in everything.

Everything in creation is part of the one.
In all the planets, stars, moon, and sun;

The oceans, the sky, and every land;
And all living things, you will find his hand.

The Path

Each life we live starts with a pact,
The things we must do and the way we must act.
Each task we take on will nourish the soul.
Spiritual improvement is the ultimate goal.

We have all agreed to the tasks we perform,
And each soul's evolution is born in the storm.
Nothing you have promised will ever pass you by.
Nothing promised to you will ever fade or die.

Each task must be met and then completed,
But some poor souls will be bowed and defeated.
Those failed tasks must be met once again,
With all of their hardship and all of the pain.

But then no one will travel a lonely path,
And there is never punishment or God's wrath.
There is spiritual guidance at every turn,
And as spirit ourselves, we move forward and learn.

The mistakes we make are to be expected,
But we have helpers and guides, so no one's neglected.
And at the end of each life, we are homeward bound
With all that experience and truth we have found.

It's a time of joy with family and friends
In a place of contentment where love never ends.
The great spirit's flame will never stop burning,
And an everlasting life means we never stop learning.

Thank God

The stars that live in the heavens;
the flowers in the wild;
The birds and the bees;
The birth of a child;

The trees that give us shade;
Vegetables in the ground;
The sun that helps with growth—
God's wonders all around.

Insects to pollinate the flowers;
Fruit on bushes and trees;
And rainfall when we need it,
But don't overdo it please.

Music for our pleasure;
Family and friends;
The loyalty of a pet;
And love that never ends.

The wind with all its power;
The clouds that pass us by;
Knowledge of the spirit world;
And knowing we cannot die.

The agony and the ecstasy
That is life and all its glory;
the harsh lessons I've had to learn,
But that's another story.

God's creatures all around us;
Fish in rivers and the sea;
And the thing that I'm most grateful for:
God found you both for me.

Share the Planet

Do we really think what's happening now
Is such a big surprise?
How our weather is radically changing
Before our very eyes?
This planet is suffering badly,
Being abused by the greed of man.
So nature is trying to open our eyes
In the only way she can.

We call them natural disasters.
They cause loss of life each day.
It's not our fault what's happening.
It's an act of God, we say.
We shouldn't ignore these changes,
Because our planet in paying the cost.
There's a new disaster almost every day,
And so many lives being lost.

Why accuse God when bad things happen
When we humans are to blame?
It's never ever our fault,
And it's always been the same.
Mother Nature may have found a cure,
Because human greed is a raging disease,
And with the help of all the elements,
She can bring us to our knees.

Remember, we are just one life-form
On a planet. We're supposed to share
With animals, birds, fish, and insects.
As humans, let's start to care.
So let's treat Mother Nature with love

On this planet of our physical birth
Before human beings cease to exist
On this rock that we call Earth.

Unconditional Love

I've come to speak with you again, Father. It's Gareth. Remember me?
I'm the guy with no hair and glasses, and I have put on weight, as you can see.
No, I haven't come to ask for anything. I've come to thank you again,
For soothing my troubled mind and helping to ease the pain.

It's been a while since we last talked, Father, and I'm sorry it's been so long.
But I'm feeling a little better now; you could almost say I'm feeling strong.
I'd like to apologize for the way I behaved, though grief plays tricks with the mind.
Thank you for being so patient with me, and thank you for being so kind.

I know you can't answer everyone's prayers, and grief enters everyone's life.
I'm sorry I got so angry with you after the loss of my wife.
And when I think back to those terrible days, when I lived my life in the dark,
I can remember seeing that first ray of light, lit by your heavenly spark.

You know what I went through, Father, and without you I wouldn't be here.
I could never have made it on my own; there was far too much pain and fear.
But you got me through the worst of it and put me back on my feet.
And to know you still watch over me makes my new life taste so sweet.

Everyone goes through the bad times, and when we do, you're at our call.
And it's not just me that you care for; you love and watch over us all.
And when we're over the worst of our pain, we forget who got us through.
We forget who listens to all our prayers, but that never bothers you.

That's called unconditional love, and it's given completely free.
There is no charge for this kind of love, and that's what you gave to me.
When you've received unconditional love, nothing else compares with this.
It's the sort of love we should all be giving, and it feels like an angel's kiss.

We Take Nothing with Us

Will we miss the song of the whale
And the dolphins that live in the sea?
Will we grieve for the death of our oceans?
And how sad will we all be?

When we've poisoned every waterway
And only acid rain falls from the sky,
Will we finally realize our mistakes?
Before or after our oceans die?

Will the rainforest have to go?
Or will we eventually see some sense?
Will we learn to do the right thing,
Or will we just sit on the fence?

Will our world finally become silent
When there's nothing able to soar in the sky
And our forests and jungles are empty?
Will that bring a tear to your eye?

Will man always succumb to greed,
Or will he one day realize
That we can't take anything with us
On the day of our so-called demise?

We fill our homes with things we don't need
That one day we will leave behind.
When we make our inevitable journey back home,
We take nothing but our spirit, soul, and mind.

For this is all we really need
After passing our final test.
Our memories, though, will be priceless
And heavenly love will supply all the rest.

When Life Comes to the Earth

Our lives are just like the seasons,
And springtime is all about rebirth.
That deathly cold winter has come to an end,
And life again will come to the earth.

It rushes in so full of hope
And learns more each and every day,
Pure and unsullied at life's onset
And fearless in every way.

As children, we don't see any danger.
We only see an opportunity to play.
And many still have that connection to spirit,
But it will lessen day by day.

In the summer of our life, we become much stronger,
Never giving a thought to old age,
Making and learning by our mistakes,
So eager to turn the next page.

Many will become more responsible now,
For they have created new life of their own,
Watching in wonder and unable to believe
The beauty of the seed they have sown.

But we carry on making mistakes,
And we learn about love and pride,
Hopefully passing some wisdom on
And missing some souls who have died.

Then in the autumn of our lives,
We look back on our many mistakes,
Regretting some things that were left undone.
This is a path that everyone takes.

We will all have some regrets,
No matter what we say,
And this is a time when many become thoughtful,
Sometimes wishing their lives away.

But this can be a good time, too.
Fond memories can make you smile
While you enjoy the laughter of grandchildren
Or just relax for a while.

Then as our winter years draw on,
We become very proud of our age.
We are no longer strong and vibrant,
But many will have the wisdom of the sage.

We will have witnessed so much of life
Evolving while here on this earth,
Having learned from life's harsh lessons
And discovering our own self-worth.

But we should still enjoy life to the fullest
Because time will now be flying.
So never sit around waiting for the end,
And don't be afraid of dying.

Life doesn't just come to an end.
We return home free from all pain,
Knowing that springtime is just around the corner,
When life will come to the earth once again.

To Become Dust

All the pain that we endure,
All the anguish and all the hurt,
All that love and all the joy,
Just to end being covered by dirt.
All the loved ones we leave behind,
All those times we succeed or crash,
All the good times and all the bad,
Just to be burnt and end as ash.
All the tears and all the suffering,
And all the caring and trust,
And it's all to no avail
Because we all just turn to dust.
How can anyone really believe this,
That we just cease to be
After everything that we go through?
It seems such a terrible waste to me.
Do you think that the power that created this universe
Would make such a huge blunder?
To waste all the knowledge we gather?
You know this really makes me wonder.
Are human beings really that stupid?
To believe that the ultimate being
Could make such a huge mistake
When he's all knowing and all seeing?
There are universal laws at work
That our father has set in stone
So that we will all live many lifetimes
And we never die alone.
For death is really a new beginning,
Free from all pain and strife,
After traveling home to the world of spirit
To begin a much better life.

Wake Up You're Not Dead

Wake up, Charlie. You're not dead.
Open your eyes, you fool.
It's no use pretending not to hear me.
Stop acting like a tool.
I must be dead. I know I am.
I was hit by a bloody great train,
And I don't believe in an afterlife.
But now I'm confused. I didn't feel any pain.
Well, I whipped you out of your body, Charlie,
A split second before impact.
And before you ask, I'm your guardian angel.
Yes, you do have one. That's a fact.
No, I still refuse to believe.
I'm an atheist, I'll have you know.
That's no excuse for being stupid.
Come with me, Charlie. We need to go.
Okay, then. Maybe I am still alive.
But where do we have to be?
Well, there is no hell, so it must be heaven.
Stop asking silly questions and follow me.
My God, that light is so strong.
Oh no, I'm floating up to the sky.
Yeah, just don't look down till I tell you, Charlie.
I told you before: you didn't die.
Will I meet my stepmother in heaven?
Please tell me she won't be there.
She scared me witless for twenty years,
And she was a kleptomaniac I swear.
Was she a big lady with tattoos on both arms?
Yeah, I do believe she's waiting in line.
She didn't look very pleased when I saw her.
No, I'm just kidding, Charlie. It'll all be fine.
Oh my God, so this is heaven.
I've never seen anything like this.

Your family and friends are coming, Charlie.
And your aunty Marge wants to give you a kiss.
Mom and Dad, you're looking great.
Aunty Rose, your leg's grown back.
Uncle Will, you have all your teeth again,
And none of them are black.
Aunty Betty, wow, you look so young.
Uncle Jack, you're a lucky devil, I swear.
The last time I saw Betty, she was ninety-six
And was looking a bit worse for wear.
There's someone else who's come to see you, Charlie.
She's just come to say hello.
Her name is Doris, and she has tattoos on her arms.
Oh my God, not her. Oh no.
It's all right, Charlie, all is forgiven.
We all try to change up here.
We see the error of our ways,
So there's no need to have any fear.
It's all right for you, mate. You're an angel.
I don't trust this woman. She was bad
She often put laxatives in my food,
And I'm sure she did the same to Dad.
We spent hours on the toilet.
We each had to take it in turn.
And every time I think of this woman,
My backside starts to burn.
Come on, Charlie. It's time to forgive.
You can't hold a grudge forever.
Well, Doris shook my hand and kissed my cheek,
And I thought to myself, Well I never.
But when she left, I counted my fingers
And was very relieved to find none were missing.
I still don't trust that woman, you know,
And she's still the last person I'd ever want to be kissing.

The Forgiven

This is a very strange world, indeed, that each of us must live in,
Where people are considered weak just for the act of forgiving.

But forgiveness is a blessing, for both the receiver and the giver.
After forgiving, your life will change. It will flow gently like a river.

To forgive someone will warm your heart and bring the recipient pleasure.
Forgiveness is a wonderful gift; forgiveness is a treasure.

But some people can't or won't forgive. They cloak themselves in hate,
Hanging on to the bitterness, sealing their own fate.

But they are only hurting themselves, you see, poisoning heart and mind,
Letting those old wounds fester when it would be easier to be kind.

There's enough hate in this world without holding on to some old grudge.
Why not offer the olive branch instead of saying, "I'm not going to budge?"

There isn't a wound that can't be mended; there isn't a hurt too sore to heal.
All you need to do is say, "I forgive," and see how good that makes you feel.

And if your hand is not accepted, at least you've done your part
By holding out that hand of friendship and opening up your heart.

And when you've let go of your anger, you will feel as light as air.
The pain will finally disappear as if it were never there.

Forgiveness is a gift from God, and it's in every human heart.
All we must do is find it and then allow the healing start.

The God of Love

One man says we're all brothers and sisters.
The other threatens with a gun or a knife.

One man says give peace a chance.
Then the other man takes his life.

Which one is following God's true path?
The one for peace or the one who wants war?
The one who tries to be spiritual
And says what are we fighting for?

Or is it the one who is so full of anger,
And wishes to have power over others,
Willing to do anything for this power,
Even killing his sisters or brothers?

If you only care about yourself
And worry about no one else at all,
If you follow an angry and violent path,
Then you are heading for a fall.

There are so many people today
Who only follow their own hedonistic path,
And they don't believe in a God at all,
Or if they do, then it's a God of wrath.

We all need to open our eyes
Because we all serve the same loving master,
And thinking that he is a vengeful God
Is just flirting with disaster.

We are all a part of the one true God,
But some religions convey a different word.
And if your religion tells you to kill,
Then the truth you haven't heard.

Why do you believe in a savage God?
And the one who taught you to kill in his name?

Why do you follow such hateful men?
And who are these men of shame?

Don't let yourself be brainwashed.
Think for yourself and follow your heart.
Lay down your weapons and anger.
Follow love's path and make a fresh start.

The one true God is all-forgiving,
But the false one is so full of dread.
I believe in a God of unconditional love,
And I refuse to believe that my God is dead.

So many believe in this angry God,
And they believe in an eye for an eye.
They only care about vengeance
And are willing to murder, cheat, or lie.

I believe if you live by the sword,
You will perish in the very same way.
You may have power and wealth for a while,
But in the end you will have to pay.

Don't you see that you are being manipulated
Like puppets on a string, without free will,
Given a gun, a rifle, or a bomb
And told you will have your reward when you kill.

It's time to end the hate and the violence,
And please stop following like so many sheep.
Wake up and smell the coffee, my brothers.
It is so much better than staying asleep.

A Pathway

There are many roads that lead to God,
But each pathway is strewn with thorns.
Though after you've finally seen his light,
That's when a new day dawns.
It will bring great changes in you
That others will clearly see.
Fear of death will eventually fade,
And another soul will be set free.

You will start to become your higher self.
These changes will be steady and strong.
You will become far more aware
That this was meant for you all along.
Once spirit has shown you the way,
The rest is up to you,
Though spirit will always guide you
In all that you say and do.

All you need do is listen
To the voice that's always been there,
Trying to help you through the bad times
That have often seemed so unfair.
But eventually you will understand
That this is how it was meant to be,
For we grow through all our hardship
Until death can set us free.

Free from a body that weighs us down,
Free from earthly lies,
To soar as a being of pure light
That never ever dies.
A spirit set free at last

Without any pain, anger, or fear.
Then we totally become our higher self
With the knowledge that God has always been near.

Stay on Your Path

When you finally begin to understand
That the path you are on has already been planned
And that coincidence has never existed at all,
That's when all your old beliefs will fall.

Déjà vu may be places you've seen,
Maybe shown to you in a dream,
Or it might be a scene from another past,
A previous life being revealed at last.

Intuition comes from your soul,
Helping to guide you, and that's the goal,
Trying to keep you on the right road
And always helping to lighten your load.

Then there's that voice inside your head.
That's spirit leading you where you need to be led,
And that sudden idea that will light your fire,
That's spirit, too. This is how they inspire.

We do have freedom of choice. This is true.
But spirit is there just to help you.
The more you listen, the fewer mistakes you make.
And being fully aware is all it will take.

So don't ever think you're on your own.
They see every seed that you've ever sown.
There's a link of love that cannot end
And will never let you down, my friend.

A Prayer to Heaven

The barrier between life and afterlife
Is very tenuous, indeed.
Our lost loved ones are only a breath away
And are always there when we are in need.

When you become more aware
And are sensitive enough to see
What many others have no idea about,
Then you'll probably be full of wonder like me.

I wish everyone could see what we see,
Hear what we hear, and feel what we feel,
To know we are all God's children
And that death has never been real.

It would change mankind forever,
Knowing there is one God who sees all.
Knowing that we are all his children
And that he will never let us fall.

Knowing there's a better life to come
After this earthly hell.
Knowing that only the body dies
Because after all, it's only a shell.

Knowing that every bad deed is seen
And that every good one is noted, too.
Do you think we'd be a bit kinder then
And more caring in what we say and do?

Do you think we would then understand
That hate should be left behind,
That envy, greed, and anger are wrong,
And that love is the path we need to find?

Gareth W. Phillips

You know, if everyone was truly equal
And color didn't matter at all
And power was unable to corrupt us,
Then all our barriers would have to fall.

If no one was able to feel superior
And look down their nose at others,
If the ego was seen for what it really is,
Maybe we'd realize we're all sisters and brothers.

No one would have to starve
If greed was a thing of the past.
Then peace on earth would truly be found,
Bringing an end to war at last.

Maybe one day this could all happen
If the blind stop leading the blind.
So pray that our leaders are selfless not selfish.
Then a heaven on earth we may find.

Maybe this is all just a pipedream,
Though some dreams do come true.
But we are all responsible for this world we live in,
So the changes must start with me and with you.

CHAPTER17

Numerology

Gawain and the Grail Quest

During one of Madeline's visits in the latter half of 2013, she asked me what my middle name was. When I told her it was Wayne, for some unknown reason she started laughing. Madeline had always shortened my first name to Gar, and while she was laughing, she put the two names together and came up with Garwayne before she changed it again to Gawain, and then she laughed even louder. I just stood there watching her with a grin on my own face until I suddenly realized that the previous day she had given me a spiritual catalog called the *Cygnus Review*. I remembered that I had seen a book there called *Gawain and the Grail Quest written by Jeffrey John Dixon*.

From a very young age I had been interested in the Arthurian tales, in which the name Gawain is often mentioned as one of King Arthur's greatest knights. As someone who doesn't believe in coincidence and has been given so many spiritual messages through books, I was not surprised when I purchased this book and found the message that I was looking for on page 180:

> Human civilization is faced by a global threat potentially far more devastating than any act of terrorism. The progressive destruction of our natural environment of which global warming is merely the tip of the iceberg. And with the melting of the polar ice caps, we are warned, there will come a new deluge that threatens to drown

our world as an earlier human race, according to Middle Eastern mythology. Fear death by water, will God breathe again upon the face of the deep?

This was confirmation of an earlier message I had received about the disasters that await humankind in the future. Not only have I been warned many times about the environmental disasters to come, but I have also been told that water will play a huge part in them. I wrote the following poem while in an altered state, and all I did was write what I was told to write. After I had finished this poem, I couldn't think what to call it. Then suddenly I heard someone say, "After the flood."

After the Flood

All people of the earth, hear what I say.
The time is very near for your judgment day.
The winds will blow, and much rain will fall.
Then thoughts of the ark mankind will recall.
The heavens will open to reveal the flood,
And the earth will be stained by mankind's blood.
Then a world torn asunder by the earth's shaking
Will see tears of the homeless and hearts breaking.
A time is coming that will bring disease,
And the earth's corrupt leaders will be brought to their knees.
The just will be saved, though the guilty must pay.
So the greedy and powerful will be all blown away.
Many will pass to the other side
To learn the true word of God that they always denied.
They will not be punished, for our father is kind.
All their evil will be shown and then washed from the mind.
And from the ashes of the old, a new world will arrive,
Built by the innocent, who were meant to survive.
So the meek will at last inherit the earth,
As it states in the Bible after mankind's rebirth.
Their leaders will be those who were sent from above,
With the true word of God containing only light and love.

The earth will be cleansed and will be as before.
Then all of God's creature's mankind will adore.
The birds of the air will again sing their songs
To implore all of God's children to just get along.
This new world is coming. Believe what I say.
But first, mankind must face a new judgment day.

Way before I read that passage and wrote that poem, the number 180 has been turning up regularly in my life, and I refuse to believe it is a coincidence. I worked for Pirelli for almost thirty years and in all that time my works clocking in number was always 180. Since I became a spiritualist, I have learned over time that there is no such thing as a coincidence, and any spiritualist worth his or her salt will tell you coincidences do not exist.

Numbers can have a profound meaning in our lives. Here are some more examples. After becoming interested in numerology, I looked at my first wife Tina's birthday, which was on February 18, 1952 (18/02/1952). Notice that the first three digits are 180. When I met Marie, my second wife, I did a numerology chart for her, and I discovered that her birthday fell on November 8, 1972 (08/11/1972). The first three digits are 180 reversed. As I said earlier, there is no such thing as coincidence. I have received many other signs in numerology over the years.

I met my first wife Tina on September 25, 1972, and we were married exactly eleven months later, on August 25, 1973. I started going out with Marie on October 25, 2015, and we were married two and a half years later, on May 25, 2017.

We then asked a good friend and spiritualist minister Susan Moss from Hereford to give us a spiritual blessing sometime during the following month, and it had to be during a Sunday service at our church in Aberdare. The only date she could give us was June 25, 2017. So, as you can plainly see, a pattern has emerged. Is it by coincidence? I really don't think so. There are also some special spiritual numbers in numerology. Two of the most special numbers are eleven and twenty-two. I was born on April 11, and Marie was born in November, the eleventh month. Marie and I now live in the house in which I was born, which was left to me by my aunt Margaret and my uncle Alan; that house number is—you guessed it—twenty-two.

CHAPTER 18

Even More Poems

My Pet Hates

Drivers who talk on mobile phones.
Motorways covered with red-and-white cones.
Cars in the wrong lane at roundabouts.
Swearing in public and litter louts.

Ann Robinson and her dreadful wink.
And any person who would dare to wear mink
In fact, anyone wearing a genuine fur
That would look much better on an animal than on him or her.

Religious bigots who say I'm heading for hell.
And cold callers, I dislike them as well.
Every part of my body that creaks and aches.
Most creepy crawlies, especially snakes.

Those speed bumps that are multiplying.
Most politicians, who can't stop lying.
They say it's not our fault, and they pass the blame.
It doesn't matter which party; they're all the same.

All those drivers who don't indicate,
Including the ones who do but leave it until too late.

Drivers who tailgate, now that's not funny.
And all those bankers who are rolling in our money.

Government cutbacks that affect the poor.
The rich won't be worried, that's for sure.
Testing on animals that are locked in cages.
Now that really does get me into rages.

Suicide bombers who think they're doing Allah's will
When it's really a man who has taught them to kill.
Angry bullies who are so full of spite
And usually hateful and not very bright.

Those people who believe they're a cut above.
They need to find God and learn about love.
Anyone, really, who looks down his or her nose.
Racists and bigots from their heads to their toes.

The powerful who have taken our freedom away.
Now governments are watching us more each day.
They tax you in every which way they can.
Before long, they will tax me for being a man.

So I'll have to wear skirts and pretend to be girly.
I've already thought of a name: I'll call myself Shirley.
No, I apologies for that. I've gone much too far.
And anyway, I don't fancy wearing a bra.

Then there's big brother. Oh, give me a break.
And of Jeremy Kyle, I've had all I can take.
All those reality shows on TV.
And any older man who has more hair than me.

I'll end on that note because I do need to go.
And that's all I can think of. So for now, cheerio.

Gareth W. Phillips

Advice to all Married Men

Most women want a knight in shining armor,
Not some bloke with a belly.
What they want is a Romeo,
Not someone whose socks are smelly.

So you will have to raise your standards, guys,
Or she won't be satisfied.
She will mold you into the man she wants,
And there'll be times you will wish you had died.

For there is nothing more determined
Than a woman with a plan.
What she really wants is an Adonis,
Not someone who is merely a man.

She wants a Brad Pit or a George Clooney,
Not someone who picks his nose.
She doesn't want someone scruffy.
She wants someone who smells like a rose.

She will nag you about your snoring,
But never tell her she does as well.
And never forget her birthday
Because she will rightly give you hell.

We know we have more bad habits than them.
Many of us swear or slurp our tea.
But we do have the right to burp in public
As long as we say, "Pardon me."

But now there's something important I have to say.
You don't have to be under the thumb.
It's your right to break wind if you're desperate,
Leave the seat up or scratch your bum.

So remember, men, she also has faults,
But don't tell her. Never tell the wife.
Because women have incredible memories,
And you will suffer for the rest of your life.

You will wish for the fires of hell,
So don't be stupid and do take this advice:
You had better let sleeping dogs lie.
Just suffer in silence and try to be nice.

Don't leave your clothes on the floor.
Treat her with kindness and never be rude.
Remember who's cooking your meals, guys.
She could easily slip something into your food.

So remember to bring her flowers.
Tell her you love her and always be true.
And try to understand her.
In the end, this should do.

Just remember to keep your big gob shut
Even though she's not perfect by any means.
Then she might be happy with the man she chose
And forget about the man of her dreams.

That's Fine by Me

If we could stop all the noise inside our heads and quieten that human brain,
If we could just simply listen, who knows what we would hear again?

Imagine discovering all those secrets locked away in the human soul.
We would be certain of our destiny then and understand our roll.

But if we unlocked all those secrets, everything once hidden and then shown,

Life would become much easier, but some secrets are best left unknown.

Maybe it's better the way it is. Life's mysteries are meant to be.
Would you want to know the day you will die? Well, that's not for me.

We were always meant to feel sadness. Human beings were born to cry.
We were meant to have incredible joy but never to know when we'll die.

It's natural to want to know more, and it does no harm to sit in the silence.
Dismissing the outside world for a while and ignoring its noise and violence.

And it doesn't hurt to look inward, to become aware of the soul inside.
You might see things in a different light and relinquish anger, ego, and pride

When you become more aware, more attuned to your higher being,
You will understand who you really are, like a blind man suddenly seeing.

And once your eyes have been opened, they will never close again.
Spirit will bring you out of the darkness and take you away from your pain.

I don't know where my destiny lies, but that's just fine by me.
I'm planning to take it one day at a time, and whatever will be, will be.

The Day I Met Marie

The day I met Marie
Is a day I will never forget.
I was given her name by my wife in spirit
Three weeks before we met.
I can't remember the date
Or if there was sunshine, rain, or snow.
I just remember the way she smiled,
The one I was always meant to know.
At first I thought, *This can't be her.*
She's far too young for me.

But Tina said, "Gareth, she is the one."
So I knew she had to be.
We went on to become very close friends,
And it was meant to be much more,
But sometimes fear gets in the way
And stops us from becoming sure.
But eventually it did happen,
And it was well worth the wait.
Now we're engaged to be married,
Even if it's a little bit late.
Every day I learn more about her.
Every day my feelings grow.
I want to spend my life with her,
And there's so much more I want to know.
Every day we become much closer.
Two souls are starting to blend.
Two spirits are becoming one.
Two hearts are starting to mend.
This is the way it was meant to be,
A promise made before this time.
I promised I would be Marie's forever,
And Marie said she'd be mine.

All Part of the Deal

An ever-lasting miracle
That was promised at the start,
A gift from God to all of us
That never will depart.
Everlasting life, my friends,
A promise to all mankind,
A chance to progress through learning
And the broadening of every mind.
Believe in reincarnation.
It's all part of the deal.
The growing of our consciousness

With extra senses that are so real.
But we can never move on and progress
Until a lesson is finally understood,
For sometimes we make the same old mistakes.
Then we can stall, and that isn't good.
But once we change our ways
We will always progress again
Through the learning process called life
That contains joy, happiness, and unfortunately, pain.
And at the end of each life we live,
When our earthly body has run its course,
We leave our human shell behind
And are met by a heavenly force.
So each and every life must begin
With the pain caused by our birth
And end with even more pain
For the loved ones we leave on this earth.
But if only everyone could understand
That death is never the end,
that love will last forever,
And that on God's promise we can all depend.

A Bumpy Road

Like everyone else I've had my problems.
I've had my share of pain.
But just like our life-giving sun,
I know I will rise again.
Every single bump in the road
Has left a painful mark,
But I always knew without a doubt
That the light would follow the dark.
The harshest lessons I've had to learn
Were always meant to be mine,
And I've always known that the lower I go,
The higher I'm meant to climb.

Life isn't a bowl of cherries,
And often it doesn't seem fair.
Sometimes you can't see the sun for the clouds,
But remember the sun's still there.
The lessons that we learn
Are the lessons that we need.
We are not being punished at all.
To this we've already agreed.
Into every life, some rain must fall.
But without the rain, nothing can grow,
And without these life experiences,
How on earth would we ever know?
So remember it's not just you.
You are not alone in your pain.
We are constantly being tested, friends,
So open your arms and welcome the rain.
Yes, life is full of hardship.
Everyone has grieved and cried.
But there will always be times of great joy, too.
So sit back and enjoy the ride.

Blessed

Something so pure, something so clean,
A gift from God that even man can't demean.
Love is the answer, love is the way,
That all humankind can improve every day.

Love is the answer to everyone's prayers,
Yours, mine, ours, and theirs.
Love is a comfort, a blanket to enfold.
Love is more precious than platinum or gold.

Forget about lust, envy, or greed.
The love of another is all that we need.

Whether from family, friends, or above,
We will all feel the raw power of love.

Love is a fire that burns deep inside.
Love is universal, and it can't be denied.
And while hate brings destruction on all that conspire,
Love is for those who wish to move higher.

With each life we live, our souls will expand
With the capacity for love that progression will demand.
We progress through love. This is a fact.
It's the greatest gift and the ultimate act.

So I must give thanks to God up above
Because, despite all the hardship I've been lucky in love.
And even through times when I've felt so depressed,
I've had so much love that I know I've been blessed.

The Makeover

Lord, it's me. It's Gareth again, and I've got a big favor to ask.
This is a massive problem for me, but for you it's no big task.
I've got this event I must attend, and I've got nothing decent to wear.
I know I've asked you for other things, but this is the last time I swear.

Oh, I'm delighted with the clothes, Father. Now I won't look out of place.
But now there's another big problem: these clothes don't go with this face.
I've never been happy with my ears; they're a bit on the large side.
Could you make me eyebrows darker and my mouth just a little less wide?
Oh, and while you're at it, Father, could you give me a little more hair?
Especially on the top, it is a bit sparse up there.
And I've got this problem with my eyes; the left one's a little bit lazy.
When I'm tired, it tends to close making me look a little bit crazy.
And could you make my chin a bit wider and take my wrinkles away?
Yes, Father, I need all this right now. This event is happening today.

Thank you, Father. I'm looking quite good. You've really come up trumps.
You've taken away all the lines and ironed out all my bumps.
Once again Father thank you, but I must go. I don't want to be late.
Yes, I'll let you know how I get on; you really are a good mate.

Oh, how did I get on, Father? Well, I was told I looked like Errol Flynn.
But because no one recognized me, they wouldn't let me in.
I ended up in McDonalds and had a McChicken sandwich with fries.
So, I wish I had gone as myself now instead of going in disguise.
Please, Father, one last favor. Could you change me back to how I used to be?
This really has taught me a lesson, so now I just want to be me.

The Pearl inside the Shell

Foolish men with foolish ways
Let ego rule all their days,
Though wiser men will find great wealth
By following the higher self.
But if we let the ego die,
Getting rid of me and I,
Oh, how happy we would be
If the higher self were free.
But while on earth we live this lie
Until we can let the ego die.
For now in these bodies we must dwell,
For we are the pearl inside the shell.

Once More

The rain is falling,
But why should I care?
In my heart, it's not raining
Because you are there.
It's strange how someone

Can enter your life
And take away the sadness
And grief-filled strife.
One little angel
Sent from above
Has reopened my heart,
And once more I've found love.

What If

When I believed that my life was over
And I didn't care anymore,
I lost the will to live
And hid behind my door.
But spirit was on my case,
And they wouldn't let it rest.
They let me see another world
And told me that earthly life was a test.
They took me out of myself
And showed me the spirit inside
That has lived so many lives
And can never be denied.
They showed me who I really am,
Not this body that eventually dies.
They opened my eyes completely
To earthly mistakes and lies.
My life is very different now
Because lost loved ones set me free.
I have a new life to live
With a beautiful spirit named Marie.
But what if I'd given up on my life
And finally succumbed to total despair?
I would never have met this special one
Who was waiting for me there.
I would never have known she existed.
I would never have known such love again.

I would still be wallowing in grief and self-pity
Or would have even put an end to this life of pain.
So thank you, Father, for helping me.
I wasn't in my right mind, and you knew.
Thank you for understanding my pain
And then bringing me closer to you.

Who Turned Off the Light?

Someone turned off the light again
And left me in the dark,
Extinguishing even the smallest flame,
So there wasn't even a spark.

I felt like a train that was entering a tunnel
With never an end in sight.
One minute the sun was shining,
And the next it was darkest night.

I wasn't sure if I was alone.
It was much too dark to see.
Suddenly I heard someone crying.
Then I realized it was me.

That's when I found it hard to breathe
And my head pounded like that train.
My heart felt like a block of ice,
And my tears just fell like rain.

I know this condition oh so well
And the feelings that often return,
And it's always when I'm on my own
That I seem to crash and burn.

That's when I feel the room getting colder
And someone touching my hair.

That's when the darkness starts to lift
Because I know that you are there.

And you're always there when I need you
To take away the pain.
Then that train comes out of the tunnel,
And the sun is shining again.

CHAPTER 19

Philosophy

On the pages that follow, I have included some samples of the philosophy I have written with the help of my spirit guides. I have used each and every one of these writings in churches over several years. They are separate bits of philosophy that I have often used, so some of them may repeat some of the contents of others. They are to be used as separate readings.

A Being of Light

You must cast off all negativity. You must be aware of all your dark thoughts. You are here on this earth for but a short time, and you are here to learn. You are a being of the light, so you must look to the light. While here on this earth, you have two bodies: one spirit body that remains hidden and the physical body that you know well. This outer shell is but a vehicle, a means of transport, while you are here on this earth. Your true identity lies hidden deep inside with your soul. This particular outer shell is yours for the length of this life only; it will diminish with the passage of time and will one day become part of this earth. But the part of you that cannot die will return home to a place of light and unbelievable beauty.

Like each and every one of you, I too am an immortal being who has chosen to be here at this time to learn and progress through the pain and hardship of an earthly life. But most importantly, we are here to learn about love while in the physical world. Love comes in many forms, and it can bring incredible joy, but it can also bring terrible heartache. You are here to learn from both. Unconditional love is a powerful force for good, but spiritual love is the greatest love of all. Unconditional love cannot be bought or sold; it is a flame that can never be extinguished. It will comfort you like a mother's shawl and is unquenchable and unconquerable. Love is the meaning of life. Love is life, and nothing else can compare.

If you find true love in this earthly life, you are rich beyond compare. You hold the universe in your hands and should want for nothing more. If you have earned the love of many, then you are blessed, indeed. While you are here on this earth, learn all your lessons well before you return home with all the knowledge you have gathered. And I tell you now, you cannot be harmed, for the real you that dwells deep inside is an immortal being that is part of the creator of all things. So be confident and fully aware, and then go forward with the knowledge that this life you have now is but a very pale shadow of the life that awaits you for all eternity.

Love Is Life

Every living thing that is capable of love has a soul, and any love that you have shared can never be lost. For every living thing with a soul can never die. Love endures, and love is eternal. We are here in our human form to learn about love. Every hardship we go through is designed to build our character. So we evolve through each hardship and each life we live. This builds our character and our capacity for love. Love isn't just an emotion between two human beings, and it should never be mistaken for a much baser instinct called lust. The love of a friend or a pet can be just as important to some people as the love of a family member. And each type of love you feel is essential for your growth.

The unconditional love that comes from a parent or grandparent is a wonderful thing, but there is a far greater love than this, and that is the love that our creator has for all living things. This is the ultimate love to which we all aspire; this is the reason for the journey we are on. Believe it or not, you are traveling the same path Jesus trod. The only difference is that his journey started long before ours and he has now evolved into a near perfect spiritual being. But even he is still on a journey of enlightenment.

We are all on an everlasting quest for knowledge and love, but being able to accept all of life's hardships is essential for our growth, though eventually we do reap the rewards. We have to learn from our pain and put our experiences to good use by helping others.

Every loving relationship that you have formed during your many lifetimes will one day be remembered again when you are pure spirit once more. And you will see every relative, friend, or family pet again on that happy day. Remember, life is eternal and your higher self is an eternal being, so why should anyone be afraid to die?

A Garden of Eden

Each and every one of us has problems in our lives, and because we are so preoccupied by these problems, we give little or no thought to some of the events that are happening worldwide. But as spiritual beings, there are questions we need to ask ourselves. Is our weather becoming far more unpredictable, are the seasons beginning to change, are natural disasters becoming more frequent? And are these and other problems caused by mankind's complete disregard for Mother Nature?

It's not just our changing climate that is a problem. The pollution of our oceans is also a cause of great concern. Why would schools of whales and dolphins suddenly beach themselves over and over, actually seeming to commit suicide? These are not isolated incidents. This has happened many times and in many countries. In two separate incidents, 225 dolphins beached themselves in Southern Iran and consequently died. So are our seas so polluted that these poor unfortunate creatures are suffering so much that they no longer wish to live? Or are they somehow becoming confused and disorientated by the pollution in our seas?

We dump so much rubbish and chemicals into our oceans that some parts of them are becoming almost lifeless.

Do you know where the largest rubbish dump in the entire word is situated? It's in the Pacific Ocean. There are millions of tons of garbage there, and it consists mostly of plastic. Many sea birds and mammals die each year because of plastic waste.

Ask yourself another question. Why is man destroying the rainforest when we know that trees are the biggest provider of oxygen, which is the largest component of the air we need to breathe? Trees also remove many harmful pollutants from our atmosphere. So if we keep cutting these trees down, eventually the changes to all life on this planet will be catastrophic. Trees are living things and not just a resource that mankind can use for building; we are not just talking about lifeless pieces of wood here.

The Brazilian rainforest is being cut down to provide land for crops by a country that is struggling with poverty and debt. Instead of sitting back and watching this ecological disaster take place, countries like America, Britain, France, and others should be giving the Brazilian government help to avoid this madness. We need to change our attitude toward all the other life-forms with which we share this planet and toward our treatment of the planet itself. For centuries man has interfered with the delicate balance of nature, and now the results of that interference can be seen far more clearly.

But man cannot see past his own greed, and we are failing to understand that human beings cannot eat money. The final use we may have for paper money is burning it to keep ourselves warm. If human beings fail to change the materialistic way in which we are living, we do not deserve a second chance and will eventually go the way of the dinosaur. Then maybe one day in a distant future, without the hindrance of mankind, this planet will recover and actually become a Garden of Eden.

But let us hope that man will one day turn his back on ignorance and greed and take a step back from the edge of the precipice. I really do believe that with the help of spirit we can achieve this, because we will have to.

A Lesson to Learn

The kingdom of heaven is within, we are told, because the divine spark of our creator resides within each of us. That spark is in all living things, including our Mother Earth. Everything in creation has that spark because it was created by God. And as part of the divine spirit, we are all immortal beings that move between two different dimensions. We are two beings in one. One being can only survive in the single dimension that we call the physical life, and it can only survive because of the symbiotic relationship with the being that resides within. The being that resides within can survive in both dimensions, and this is the being that can never truly know death.

Our true self is the being inside; we call this our spirit or higher self. The outer shell is just a vehicle to move around in this earthly life. And there is always a better life that awaits us when the outer shell succumbs to its inevitable fate. More and more people are beginning to realize this. We are beings of the light taking part in an everlasting journey on a quest for knowledge and progression, and we are all part of the energy we call God. When we as individuals grow, so does the one that created us. We are constantly adding to the loving energy that is creation. We are each an important part of the whole, and when we can see the connection that we have to all of creation, that's when we reach a much higher plane of development and understanding.

Each time we volunteer to return to the earth, we make promises to loved ones and ourselves. We pick the lessons we need to learn, and most of these lessons are learned through hardship and pain. But we never return alone. Some of our loved ones will go before us, and some will follow later. Each one of these beings we will meet again on our earthly visits. Some will become family, some will become friends, and others—believe it or not—will have promised to teach us lessons through pain. We will have known these beings not just in the spirit realms but also in previous lives, and we are connected to all of them through love. It's all about progression, but unfortunately, when we return for each new life, we have no memory of our past lives or the promises we have made.

At the beginning, our pathway is unclear, and this is essential to our progression, for if we knew what was ahead of us, we would be able to avoid all the painful experiences and would never successfully complete our quest.

At some point in one of our lives, we will suddenly see the light. We will have a single moment of clarity that will change our earthly life forever. But unfortunately, this will often happen after a very traumatic experience, and this is usually through the loss of a loved one. This is how it is for all of us. We are meant to sample earthly pain and pleasure. We are meant to learn about love and unconditional love, and we are meant to learn about forgiveness.

One of the biggest mistakes we can make is to return to our spiritual home never having forgiven someone for his or her mistakes. If we cannot learn about forgiveness, we will surely have to live through the same ordeal over and over again.

Remember, we are all part of the one. We are all brothers and sisters, and until forgiveness becomes second nature, we will go on making the same old mistakes.

Never forget that you have that spark of the divine inside you that connects you to our creator and to all of creation, and this makes you special. Never look in the mirror and think, *This is me. This is all that I am*, for what resides deep within you is actually your true self, your higher self that others will never see unless they make a loving connection with you, soul to soul.

As you progress spiritually, your connection to the spirit world will become much stronger. Then at some point you will move closer to being your higher self, and when this happens, the knowledge you receive will not only be coming from the spirit realms but also from deep within yourself.

There is an incredible amount of knowledge stored within your higher self that remains unobtainable until you reach that state of awareness. And when this happens, you will then be ready to be used by the world of spirit to teach your brothers and sisters who are ready to listen.

Finally, we should never return home to the Summerland with regrets for the things we never did and the things we never said. But so many of us will. So be brave. Say what's on your mind. Tell the people you love how you feel about them. It's never too late to change the way we are and the way we live our lives.

At a Crossroads

When we lose someone we love, we can become consumed by grief. One of the feelings that always seems to come closer to the surface is anger. Many of us will then find ourselves at another crossroads in life, and there seems to be two main ways we deal with this. We either start to blame God for the passing of our loved ones, or we begin to search for answers spiritually. But even if we take the wrong road, there will always be an opportunity later in our lives to alter our course. Only by keeping an open mind will we learn the truth, and we must be open to all possibilities, no matter how farfetched they seem. A closed mind will never reach a true state of awareness.

Once we start to blame God for taking a loved one from us, many of us will start to blame every bad thing we see happening in this world on the cruelty of our maker. The next step is to deny the existence of any divine being. The thing we most often hear is, "With all the terrible things happening in this world, how can there be a God?" The fact is that most of this world's tragedies are caused by human neglect, greed, or lust for power. We have abused Mother Earth for long enough, and it's about time the human race started to take responsibility for its own shortcomings.

As a spiritualist, I know we are only visiting this world to learn and evolve through our experiences in a human body, and this body is just a vehicle for our spirit and soul. Once we have learned these lessons, no matter how long or short, our souls will always return home to the spirit world, the place where we first came into being. Sometimes an old soul will come back to this earth for a very short time not to learn but to teach, and this always causes great sadness.

The lessons we learn in our earthly lives can be very painful, indeed. We will also witness great joy and earthly love, but it is the harshest lessons that teach us the most. What would we ever learn by living a life without responsibility or hardship? Absolutely nothing at all. And how many times have you heard someone say, "What doesn't kill you will make you stronger"? I can assure you that this is very true. The one thing we must never do in any of our earthly lives is start thinking like a victim, for if we think like a victim, we will become a victim. Never forget that we are cocreators while on this planet, and that means we can create our own lives through the way we think and act. So be very careful.

Eventually we will all return to our spiritual home, where we will all be nurtured and cared for in the love and light of our lost loved ones. For if there is love between spiritual beings in an earthly life, that love will live on in the afterlife.

Therefore, we should have no fear of death because what we refer to as death is just a doorway to a much better existence, and this existence will be lived without greed, envy, hate, or pain. Once you have become free of the constraints of the human body, the veil that has been placed over you will quickly be lifted. Things will then become much clearer for you, and you will not only understand why you came to earth on your most recent visit, but you will also fully absorb the lessons you have learned while in your physical form. All the memories of your past lives, whether in the physical or spirit body, will then be available to you once more, and you will understand completely who you truly are.

Your spirit, or your higher self, is the true you, the part of you that is indestructible and will know everlasting life. Your soul is your direct connection to the great spirit and to every other living thing that also has that divine connection. With each and every life we live, we become that much closer to the great spirit we call God.

I know there are an infinite number of questions and an infinite number of answers, so we will never stop evolving because there will always be more to learn.

The most important lesson that each of us will learn in time is that love is the greatest power in the universe, and unconditional love for all living things is the true pot of gold at the end of the rainbow. The meaning of life has nothing to do with personal wealth or greed; it's about love and always has been.

> *We look forward to the time when the Power of Love will replace the Love of Power. Then will our world know the blessings of peace.*

> —William Gladstone

Deep Inside Yourself

Philosophers like to talk about the meaning of life. I believe love is the true meaning of life. And to change an unhappy life, you must first change your way of thinking. It all begins by learning to love yourself. It must start with love of the self. It will then radiate outward to the love of others and eventually to the love of all living things. So if you don't love and appreciate your own inner self, you will never find true happiness. You will have to bring this love into being, or you will never move forward and evolve into the person you are meant to be. The more love you can bring into your life, the more you can change the way you think and act.

Love changes everything for the better and always has. If you feel unworthy of love, you turn your heart into a desert, and love cannot grow in a barren place. Many people who through perseverance have learned how to meditate have realized who they truly are, and they know they are as good as anyone but never better because we each have God's spark inside us. When you finally understand this, you can then start to move forward with love and light, thus changing your life and the lives of others who love you. It's all about having the confidence to believe this about yourself.

Unfortunately, in every lifetime we meet people who tell us that we are ugly, or too fat or thin, and those people have made us feel that we are a lesser than we truly are. It's these damaging messages from others that cause the negative feelings we have about ourselves.

These people like to make others feel inferior because it makes them feel superior, even if it is over just one other person, because they probably have issues of self-loathing themselves. So instead of learning to love and understand who they are, they strike out at another vulnerable person with the same problems. It's a vicious circle that could so easily be avoided through love. These problems usually start at a very young age when we are at our most malleable and vulnerable. So whether it's an adult who says that you are stupid or other children who call you skinny, fatty, or ugly, remember that it's their problem, not yours.

And if you are unhappy with something about yourself, you have only two options: (1) change what you don't like about yourself if you are able to or (2) learn to live with it and learn to love who you are no matter what others say by seeing beyond what others can see.

And remember, it could be so much worse. You could be one of those people who has an ego that is so huge and love themselves so much that no one else can love them. These people don't need enemies because they are their own worst enemy. We must never allow others to tell us who we truly are, because no one can see the real you. We are all individual beings, and we all come from the same divine spark. Your soul will always remain hidden from others, and until you start to search for yourself, it will remain partly hidden from you, too.

We are all meant to eventually understand who we truly are through the living of many lives. You are not the reflection you see in the mirror. The reflection you see in that mirror is of a human shell borrowed for this one particular lifetime. You are a being of the light that has asked for the problems you are encountering here on this planet so that you can evolve into that which you wish to be. We are all spirit, we are all connected to one another, and believe it or not, we will all live forever. Our father, God, has given us plenty of time to learn to love who we truly are, so maybe we should all get on with it.

It's Inspiration

You may not think so, but each and every one of us receives inspiration from spiritual sources. Whether this inspiration comes directly from the spirit world or from our higher selves, it doesn't matter because we are all spirit. What we think of as intuition or our own ideas are actually just as likely to have come from spirit. I believe that without the help of the spirit world, human beings would find life much harder than it is now.

Every one of us has spiritual gifts, but many have not yet begun to understand them because they are not yet aware of who they truly are. We all go through many lifetimes before becoming aware of our inner spirit or our higher self. But by becoming more aware of the spirit world and by practicing meditation, your awareness will blossom, and eventually you will find out who you really are. Then you will become more aware of your own gifts.

Each of us is inspired by spirit, whether from without or within. You may be an artist, a musician, a writer, or an inventor, but no matter where your gift lies, spirit has and always will inspire you. But many people today are not listening because they have become more and more seduced by the pleasures of this physical world and have become so unaware of the spiritual that they no longer hear the voice inside that is trying to help them find their pathway. Sometimes all it takes is the loss of a loved one to make them ask the right questions. This happens to so many of us, myself included.

By using meditation daily, we can become attuned not only to the world of spirit but to our own higher self, and through this practice we can become far more aware of our true nature. By just sitting in silence and letting our thoughts drift inward, we can learn so much about ourselves and bring about great changes in our earthly lives. I believe we have always benefited from listening to spirit, whether we realize it or not. We have also been helped to find cures for diseases and to invent things that have made human life easier on this planet. I believe spirit has always played a major part in all human achievements. Where this human race is going in the future, who knows. But one thing is certain: spirit will always try to illuminate our pathway.

The Natural Laws of the Universe

The natural laws of the universe are perfect, and we as beings of the light live all our many lives in a constant movement toward perfection. The very fact that we are currently here on this planet means we are still striving for perfection. If we do not learn from the mistakes we make while we are here on this earth, we will be given the opportunity to make the same mistakes again. Until we learn the lessons from our mistakes, we do not move on to the next vital lesson in another lifetime.

We become stuck on a treadmill that leads to nowhere. The lessons we are meant to learn are there right in front of us. They are not hidden from our view. But often we stubbornly ignore them. Oh, if only we could comprehend that every time we refuse to love, understand, or forgive we climb back onto the treadmill once again. We must realize that it's not just about being taught a painful lesson; it's about learning from that experience.

Every time we end one of our lives with hate and resentment still in our hearts, we go back to the same old life with the same painful lessons that we really don't want to go through again. When we enter a new life, we will not know what is in front of us. Our lessons are hidden so that we can learn from our own experiences and end that life with forgiveness, understanding, and love at the center of our being. Only then do we move onward and upward. Only then do we climb the ladder of perfection. Only then do we become one with the universe and its natural laws.

The Human Condition

Part 1: The Ego

We are spirit beings visiting this earthly world of separation, where we all go through the process we think of as our human existence. But as spirit beings we are all connected to each other and to our creator while we are in our true home on the other side of the veil. But this separation is needed for growth while on the earth plane.

Whenever we feel the need to sample another earthly life for our progression, we will need our human outer shell in order to understand the physical experiences that will hasten our spiritual progress, because of the difficulties we must all face inside our human form.

When we first come back to the earth, most of us are disconnected from our fellow spirit beings in the higher realms and on the earth. The first and most important connection we will all make is with our mother, followed by our father and the rest of our family and friends. We then go through the rest of our physical lives making new connections and periodically losing some others, unfortunately.

While on the earth, we are driven by a force called the ego, which we need to learn and evolve in our earthly lives, but if the ego is too strong, we can make problems for ourselves. The trick is not to be totally dominated by our own ego. If we let our ego dominate our lives, then we become too self-possessed and selfish. We must learn to control our ego and not let it control us. If we are able to do this, then we become more loving, caring people and are able to let our lives flow without too much hindrance.

Part 2: Loving Yourself

You are perfect, and you were created by the loving energy that we call God. We all carry his divine spark within. While on this planet, you will be living the life you asked for, whether you believe it or not. But you have been given free will, and this free will can often be the cause of our mistakes. But then again, we are all meant to make mistakes and learn from them before returning to the light.

We must all remember that it doesn't matter how many times you have been brought to your knees; it's how you react that counts, picking yourself up, dusting yourself off, and starting all over again. And one of the most important things you need to remember is that you are not who other people say you are. You are here to live the life you promised to live, not the life someone else wants you to live.

You are the cocreator of your own life, and you are a spirit being here on this planet for the evolution of your immortal soul. The body you have been loaned for this life is less than perfect, unlike the inner being that is the true you. The real you will outlive every human body that you will ever be given. So when someone tells you that you are not perfect because you are too fat or too thin or that you are ugly or stupid, remember that the shining being that resides within is the real you, not the mortal outer shell. You must not let another person's opinion of you affect you at all.

Many of us are affected during childhood by someone who has taken it upon him – or herself to tell us that we are not worthy, and many of us will carry this terrible burden into our adult lives because we have given too much credence to other people's spiteful words. But then these spiteful people usually behave the way they do because they feel inadequate themselves and stupidly believe that by running someone else down, it will advance their own superiority. This is actually a by-product of their own low self-worth, which was probably caused by someone who did the very same thing to them.

It is a vicious circle that never seems to end for many people, so if we can avoid doing to others what has been done to us, we do not become part of the circle of spite. We must concentrate on who we know we are inside and ignore all hurtful comments. It's not easy to do, I know, but we must try.

We need to remember that it's who we are inside that counts, not the mortal outer shell that will one day be discarded and left behind. We are not what we see in the mirror. We were created by the perfect source of energy, love, and light that we call God, and that energy is incapable of making mistakes.

You must learn to accept the roll you have chosen for yourself in this life and never waste your time wishing you were someone else or putting yourself down, for this is a total waste of your valuable energy and will cause you even more pain. Stand tall and believe in yourself and you will grow into the person you were meant to be. Never let other people's opinions of you affect you in the slightest way, for they have never met the higher being that is deep inside you.

This role that you are supposed to play as the cocreator of your own life must become your main priority.

You must also try to let others learn by making their own mistakes whenever possible. We cannot live other people's lives for them completely, for it will do them no good in the long run and may even hamper their progress. They must live the lives they asked for and by doing so enhance their own souls. Life is far too short, so live it to the fullest extent of your ability, and let love and forgiveness be your guide. Remember, you are a being of the light that has chosen to be in this dark and heavy world for your spiritual progression before returning to that wonderful place from whence we all came.

Learn to love yourself and then your love will radiate outward to others far more easily.

CHAPTER 20

Just a Few More Poems

All I Want for Christmas

Christmas is coming,
And the goose is getting fat,
But all I want this year
Is a certain someone in my flat.

I don't want anything expensive
Or anything smart to wear.
I don't care what's on the TV
As long as she is there.

So please no snow for Christmas
Because that could keep us apart.
So, father, be kind with the weather,
For it really would break my heart.

I don't need two front teeth.
I have enough of my own.
I don't want an Xbox or tablet,
And I don't need a mobile phone.

I don't want any chocolates
Or presents under my tree,

And you can stuff the turkey.
All I really want is Marie.

A Time for Celebration

When my time on earth comes to an end
And this human shell is cast aside,
My soul will be free from the constraints of this body,
And in celestial realms my spirit will abide.

Pain will no longer exist for me,
For I will no longer have flesh and bone.
Death will actually set me free
And allow me to finally make my way home.

This will be a time for celebration, not tears.
This is the truth I wish all could know.
Then fear of death would disappear
And spiritual knowledge would thrive and grow.

Why should we fear going home,
Back to the place where we came into being?
It's a far better place than this, I know,
And our heaven is really worth seeing.

Only when we're free from this human shell
Will we completely understand
That this earth is just a place for learning
And that the spirit world is our true homeland.

If you've understood what I'm saying
And you believe this to be true,
Then you've come to a point in your evolution
When God's light will shine through you.

And now that you've seen his light,
Don't keep the truth to yourself.
This knowledge is worth far more than gold,
So go forward and share the wealth.

A Turkey's Life

A turkey's life is a sad one.
They have no idea of their fate.
Suddenly Christmas comes along,
And they end up stuffed on a plate.

Sprouts, carrots, and cabbage,
Roast spuds and parsnips as well,
Sage and onion with sausage meat—
This is a turkey's hell.

But Gerald was no ordinary turkey.
He was very aware of his fate.
So he found a very good hiding place
And lived a long life, which was great.

When the other turkeys arrived each year,
Gerald would suddenly appear.
Every year he had the pick of the females,
And no one would put any herbs up his rear.

Gerald was well fed, and his life was good,
But he hated old farmer Ted
Because he knew what Ted was up to,
So he wished the old farmer were dead.

Gerald lived to a ripe old age.
He was a very tough old bird, you might say.
But nothing lasts forever,
And one day sadly he did pass away.

Farmer Ted found him the next morning
And thought, *Waste not, want not, you know.*
So Gerald ended up in the oven after all,
Cooked with the gas on quite low.

When Gerald came out of the oven
All crisp and golden brown,
Ted drooled with anticipation.
He couldn't wait to gobble Gerald down.

Ted took his first mouthful of Gerald,
But the meat was stringy and tough.
And a big piece of the old bird got stuck in Ted's throat,
And he started to feel a bit rough.

He gasped for air as his face changed color—
Dark pink and then purple after red.
Then farmer Ted fell flat on his face.
The grumpy old bugger was dead.

And as Ted's soul left his body
On its journey to a far better place,
He thought he saw a ghostly turkey by the door
With a huge silly grin on its face.

To the old farmer's surprise, he was still alive,
But then who was that dead on the ground?
And why did that turkey look so happy,
Dancing and prancing around?

Then as Ted started to enter the light,
He knew he wasn't alone.
And he was quite shocked to hear the old turkey say,
"Come on, you old fart. Let's go home."

A World without Love

Living within this universe without any love would be a curse,
Like living in a foreign land without someone there to hold your hand
Or playing patience or solitaire, because you know there's no one there.
Having to always make dinner for one is no one's idea of having fun.

What if we all had to live like this, never knowing the joy of love's first kiss?
Having no one at all by your side because the human need for love had died?
What a terrible way to live a life, without a husband, without a wife.
Without friends and family to lighten your load, all life on earth would just implode.

Love can make you float on air, knowing that there's someone there.
Friendship is love. That's a fact. And giving your love is the ultimate act.
Love is the reason we all endure, and if nothing else of this I'm sure.
Love is the reason we're all alive. We need to feel loved just to survive.

Though sometimes we jump before we are ready instead of taking it slow and steady.
We can pay the price for moving too fast, and that's when love doesn't seem to last.
But living as an island isn't wise; eventually tears will fill your eyes.
Never give in, there's always a chance that you will again find romance.

It's in the lyrics of most every song: a world without love would be so wrong.
And for those who only live for lust, one day your soul may turn to dust.
Sex without love may at first be thrilling, but in the end, it's unfulfilling.
Love is a seed that must be planted, so never take someone's love for granted.

Love of a friend or a family pet is also important, so never forget.
Don't close your heart if you're hurt again. Just remember, hope should always remain.

For love can always return, you know, those wonderful feelings that help us grow.
For there is nothing that can compare with being in someone's heart and staying there.

Balance and Love

We all have a need for balance in our lives,
Physical and spiritual, hand in glove,
Side by side in equal measure,
But balance can't exist without love.
The world we live in is out of balance.
Mankind is haunted by greed.
We take without any thought of giving.
We're taking far more than we need.
We can't see beyond the physical pleasures.
We don't see, hear, or feel spirit around.
All we need is a remote control
And one finger to turn up the sound.
We've forgotten how to listen.
We're forgetting how to feel.
We actually believe what the media tell us
When so much of it isn't real.
They feed us with endless lies,
And for many this world is unfair
Because so many are starving
And those in power really don't care.
But as long as we have our digital toys,
Xboxes and Sky TV,
We'll sit there in a trance.
How stupid can we be?
They numb our minds with triviality
So we don't see the corruption and lies.
We don't even realize that we are in slavery,
But now it is time to open our eyes.
There's a revolution coming

And spirit is leading the fight
Against all the powers of darkness.
Maybe then we will see the light.

I Wish I Had Wings

I was on the verge of insanity after the death of my wife.
I stayed at home and stared at walls, praying for an end to my life.
Suicide is painless; I kept hearing that song in my head.
So then I did something really stupid, and that's how I ended up dead.

While I was falling to my death, I thought of many things,
Like I wish I hadn't jumped, and oh, for a pair of wings.
That's when I realized I wanted to live, but by then it was far too late.
I knew I'd made a terrible mistake by sealing my own fate.

It's not the fall that kills you; it's the contact with the ground.
And I'll never forget that sudden pain or that awful sound.
Well, I ended up in heaven, much to my surprise,
Where I was told I must repeat this life after seeing my death through other eyes.

I had to watch my loved ones suffer and the others I had hurt.
I watched them lower my coffin down and then cover it with dirt.
I was shown someone I had been destined to meet, but now she was all alone.
We were supposed to live a good life together. If only I had known.

So this one act of selfishness caused so much sorrow.
It impacted so many lives, and it changed someone's tomorrow.
None of us know our future, and the lives that we change, who can tell?
And because I ended my own life, I have damaged others as well.

This earthly life is not ours to take, for it can change many other lives, too.
Some people say suicide is a mortal sin, but we will still go to heaven. It's true.

For there is no such place as hell. Hell is the life we live on earth.
And we must survive the life we asked for, and live it for all we are worth.

I can see all this now in hindsight, but back then I was dealing with grief.
My mind was no longer my own. It was stolen by death, that pitiless thief.
Now I must pay a forfeit by helping others who are in the same state
Before living my last life again, hopefully this time with a far different fate.

A Whisper

I once spoke to Jesus, and then Jesus spoke back.
He said, "You took your time, but now you're on the right track."
He said, "Avoid all dogma and religion's mistakes.
Just sit in the silence, and that's all it takes."
"God is within you. He's been there from the start
So, listen to your soul, and follow your heart."
He said, "I am God's son, but then so are you.
We are all his children. I promise it's true."

I then spoke to Mohamed, and Mohamed said,
"Spirit can't die, so the dead are not dead."
He said, "You've talked to the Nazarene, my friend and my brother.
Now you know we're connected, everyone to another.
We're all brothers and sisters. Now you have the proof.
We are all equally loved, and this is the truth."
I didn't understand this when I was earthbound,
For we all make mistakes, but now the truth I have found.

I next spoke to Buddha, and Buddha just smiled.
He said, "There's nothing more precious than an innocent child."
He said, "Ignore all color, and ignore all creed.
Then let go of any anger, envy, or greed."
He said, "Do away with the ego. Wave it good-bye.
Set your higher self free. Just give it a try."
He said, "Brother killing brother, this isn't God's way.
So mankind may be taught a harsh lesson one day."

I then prayed to God and thanked him for life.
I thanked him for the love of friends, family, and wife.
I thanked him for the knowledge that I came here to learn,
And I thanked him for the progression that I hope to earn.
I prayed, "Father, let me serve you in any way I can.
For I now know I'm spirit and not just a man.
My awareness has grown, so I know I'm your son."
Then a voice whispered gently, "Gareth, well done."

I Gave You Life

I gave you life
To do as you please,
For you to stand tall
Or to drop to your knees.
I gave you my blessings.
I created you all.
I gave you free will.
To rise or to fall.

There's a spark inside you
That was once part of me.
I gave it freely.
Now we shall see.
Will you tell lies,
Or will truth be your creed?
Will you be greedy
Or just take what you need?

Will you be jealous
Or maybe content?
Are you able to say sorry,
Or will you never repent?
Can you forgive,
Or will you always send hate?

Remember, my children,
You control your own fate.

I worry about my children
In these troubled times.
I see wickedness and violence.
I see perversion and crimes.
I can see all your wars
Created by greed
And the lust for power
That you don't really need.

This life is fleeting.
It doesn't last long.
I hoped you would learn,
But maybe I was wrong.
You are destroying the earth
And its creatures as well.
Can't you see the mayhem?
You've created a hell.

Many people don't care now.
The self is the master.
They are driven by their egos
And heading for disaster.
I wanted you to grow
With every life you live.
I wanted you to care.
I wanted you to give.

Have you forgotten who I am?
Has your connection been derailed?
Do you only serve mammon?
So have I now failed?
I gave you your freedom,

But you don't comprehend
That love is the answer
And that's all you should send.

The Final Word

If there is someone you know who doesn't like you,
Or even worse they hate you.
And you have done nothing to deserve their dislike or their hate,
Then there can only be one answer.
Jealousy, and that is their problem not yours.

Printed in the United States
By Bookmasters